O.D. Case & Company

The United States

historical, descriptive, and statistical, with an alphabetical index to

counties, mountains, lakes, rivers, &c.

O.D. Case & Company

The United States
historical, descriptive, and statistical, with an alphabetical index to counties, mountains, lakes, rivers, &c.

ISBN/EAN: 9783337302306

Printed in Europe, USA, Canada, Australia, Japan

Cover: Foto ©Andreas Hilbeck / pixelio.de

More available books at **www.hansebooks.com**

The United States:

Historical, Descriptive, and Statistical;

with an

Alphabetical Index

to

Counties, Mountains, Lakes, Rivers, &c.

to accompany

Case's Map of the United States.

HARTFORD:
Published by O. D. Case and Company.
CHICAGO:
A. H. Andrews & Co.
1877.

PUBLISHER'S NOTE.

The following pages have been prepared to accompany Case's Map of the United States, with a two-fold object. First, to greatly facilitate the labor of searching for details, by reference to an Alphabetical Index to Counties, Mountains, Lakes, Rivers, etc.; Second, to furnish in a condensed form a collection of important historical and geographical facts, pertaining to the United States, which can only be found widely scattered elsewhere. In the brief synopsis of facts given relative to the acquisition of territory, surface, early history, and climate, it is believed that much of the information will be found very convenient and valuable for reference, not only by those who have frequent occasion to consult maps, but by others also.

Extracts from the Government Reports of Dr. F. V. Hayden, Dr. J. S. Newberry, and Major J. W. Powell, descriptive of the Yellowstone Park, the Cañons of the Colorado River, and of Ancient Lake Basins, have also been introduced, and will be found to contain much that is interesting upon that portion of our country west of the Mississippi.

HARTFORD, August, 1876.

TABLE OF CONTENTS.

	Page.
Publisher's Note,	3
I. POSITION AND EXTENT OF THE UNITED STATES,	7
II. TERRITORY, WHEN, HOW, AND OF WHAT POWERS ACQUIRED,	8
Territory ceded by England,	8
do. do. do. France,	9
do. do. do. Spain,	10
Texas as annexed,	10
Territory ceded by Mexico in 1848,	10
do. do. do. do. do. 1853,	10
III. SURFACE,	11
1. THE EASTERN PORTION,	
The Atlantic Highland,	11
The Atlantic Plain,	12
Basin of the Great Lakes,	12
2. THE WESTERN PORTION,	
The Pacific Highland,	13
The Rocky Mountains,	14
The Cascade and Sierra Nevada Mountains,	16
The Great Basin,	17
The Basin of the Columbia River,	17
The Central Basin,	17
The Sacramento and San Joaquin Valley,	17
The Willamette Valley,	18
Deserts of California,	18
The Basin of the Colorado River of the West,	19
3. THE MIDDLE PORTION,	
The Mississippi Basin,	21
Height of Land,	22
IV. YELLOWSTONE NATIONAL PARK,	23
The Yellowstone Lake,	24
Falls and Grand Cañon of the Yellowstone River,	24
Erosive Forces,	24
Hot Springs,	25
Fire Hole Valley,	27
Mud Springs,	27
Geysers,	28

		Page.
V.	CANONS OF THE COLORADO RIVER OF THE WEST,	31
	Sources of the Colorado River,	32
	A Labyrinth of River Gorges,	33
	Flaming Gorge,	34
	A Landscape of Naked Rock,	35
	Grand Cañon, a mile deep,	36
	Appearance of the Gorge from Below,	37
VI.	ANCIENT LAKE BASINS,	38
VII.	EARLY STATE HISTORY,	52
	1. Alabama,	52
	2. Alaska,	52
	3. Arizona,	53
	4. Arkansas,	53
	5. California,	53
	6. Colorado,	53
	7. Connecticut,	53
	8. Dakota,	54
	9. Delaware,	54
	10. Florida,	54
	11. Georgia,	54
	12. Idaho,	54
	13. Illinois,	55
	14. Indiana,	55
	15. Indian Territory,	56
	16. Iowa,	56
	17. Kansas,	56
	18. Kentucky,	56
	19. Louisiana,	56
	20. Maine,	57
	21. Maryland,	57
	22. Massachusetts,	57
	23. Michigan,	57
	24. Minnesota,	58
	25. Mississippi,	58
	26. Missouri,	58
	27. Montana,	58
	28. Nebraska,	59
	29. Nevada,	59
	30. New Hampshire,	59
	31. New Jersey,	59
	32. New Mexico,	59
	33. New York,	60
	34. North Carolina,	60
	35. Ohio,	60
	36. Oregon,	60
	37. Pennsylvania,	61
	38. Rhode Island,	61

		Page.
89.	South Carolina,	61
40.	Tennessee,	62
41.	Texas,	62
42.	Utah,	62
43.	Vermont,	63
44.	Virginia,	63
45.	Washington,	63
46.	West Virginia,	63
47.	Wisconsin,	63
48.	Wyoming,	64

VIII. CLIMATE,
    Table of Places having a Mean Summer Temperature of about 60° F., - - - - - 68
    Table of Places having a Mean Summer Temperature of about 65° F., - - - - - 68
    Table of Places having a Mean Summer Temperature of about 70° F., - - - - - 68
    Table of Places having a Mean Summer Temperature of about 75° F., - - - - - 69
    Table of Places having a Mean Summer Temperature of about 80° F., - - - - - 69
    Table showing Mean Temperatures in Tropical America, - - - - - - - 69
    Table showing Mean Temperature in Europe and Asia, - - - - - - - 69
    Table showing Mean Annual Amount of Moisture Precipitated in rain and melted snow, - - - 70

IX. LIST OF THE ORIGINAL THIRTEEN STATES, 74
X. TABLE GIVING THE AREA OF EACH STATE AND TERRITORY, - - - - 75
XI. ALPHABETICAL INDEX, - - - - 75
    Alphabetical List of Counties, by States and Territories, 75
    Alphabetical List of Mountains, - - - 92
    Alphabetical List of Valleys, - - - 95
    Alphabetical List of Lakes, - - - 96
    Alphabetical List of Rivers, - - - 98
    Alphabetical List of Capes, - - - 108
    Alphabetical List of Bays, - - - 109
    Alphabetical List of Islands, - - - 110

THE UNITED STATES.

I. POSITION AND EXTENT.

The United States of America, exclusive of Alaska, occupies the central portion of North America, extending from British America on the north to Mexico and the Gulf of Mexico on the south, and from the Atlantic Ocean on the east to the Pacific Ocean on the west. It lies between 24° 30' and 49° north latitude, and between 66° 45' and 124° 45' longitude west from Greenwich. It has a shore line, including indentations and projections, of about 6,860 miles on the Atlantic, 3,460 miles on the Gulf of Mexico, 2,280 miles on the Pacific, and 3,620 miles on the northern lakes. Its Mexican frontier, following the general course of the Rio Grande River, but not its windings, is about 1,600 miles in extent, and its northern boundary, passing through the middle of the Great Lakes, is about 3,650 miles.

Its greatest breadth from north to south, between the forty-ninth parallel and the most southern point of Texas, is 1,595 miles, and its greatest length from east to west, between the most eastern point of Maine and Cape Flattery, in Washington Territory, is 2,766 miles. Its shortest length from east to west, between the coast of Georgia and the coast of southern California, is 2,077 miles. New York is distant from San Francisco 2,600 miles.

8 ACQUISITION OF TERRITORY.

The total area of the United States and Territories, including Alaska, is 3,603,884 square miles, or about four-ninths of North America, and more than one-fifteenth of the entire land surface of the globe. It is surpassed in extent only by three of the great empires of the world—the British Empire, the Russian Empire, and the Chinese Empire. This area was acquired as follows:

II. TERRITORY—WHEN, HOW, AND FROM WHAT POWERS ACQUIRED.

*Square miles.

1. The Original Thirteen States and other territory, from England, by treaty, in 1783, — 827,844
2. Louisiana, from France, by treaty, in 1803, for $15,000,000, — 1,162,287
3. Florida, from Spain, by treaty, in 1819, for $5,000,000, — 68,912
4. Texas, by annexation, in 1845—Texas debt assumed by the United States, $7,500,000, — 376,163
5. California, New Mexico, etc., from Mexico, by "Treaty of Gaudalupe Hidalgo," in 1848, for $15,000,000, — 545,753
6. The "Gadsden Purchase" from Mexico, in 1853, for $10,000,000, — 45,535

Total area exclusive of Alaska, — 3,026,494

7. Alaska, from Russia, by treaty in 1867, for $7,200,000, — 577,390

Total area including Alaska, — 3,603,884

Territory ceded by England.—The territory ceded by England, comprised the Original Thirteen States, and all east of the Mississippi River, except that portion embraced within the limits of Florida, as ceded by Spain,

---

*The areas given in this table are from data obtained from the Census Reports for 1870. The total area of the United States, as here given, is 7,965 square miles less than the total area of the several states and territories, as given separately in another place, from figures furnished by the Commissioner of the General Land Office at Washington. This discrepancy arises from an unsettled question of boundary between Nevada and California, the Act of Congress defining the boundaries of Nevada having included within the limits of that state a narrow strip (7,965 square miles) of California, on condition that the latter state should assent to such change of boundary. It appears that California has never given the necessary assent, and that both states claiming the disputed strip, the Commissioner of the Land Office includes it within the area of each.

ACQUISITION OF TERRITORY. 9

which included all within the present limits of Florida, and such portions of Alabama, Mississippi, and Louisiana as are situated south of the 31st parallel.

Territory ceded by France.—Louisiana, as ceded by France, extended from the Gulf of Mexico northward, along the west bank of the Mississippi River to British America, and westward, north of the 42d parallel, to the Pacific Ocean. Its western and southern boundary was up the Sabine River to the 94th meridian, along the 94th meridian to the Red River, up the Red River to the 100th meridian, along the 100th meridian to the Arkansas River, up the Arkansas River to the Rocky Mountains, along the Rocky Mountains to the 42d parallel, along the 42d parallel to the Pacific Ocean. A small area (3,744 square miles) lying east of the Mississippi River, south and west of Lake Ponchartrain, was also included in this purchase.

Other claims to the title of this territory, besides that conveyed by France, also existed. (1.) The United States claimed all west of the Rocky Mountains, and as far north as 54° 40′, on the ground of discovery and exploration, —Capt. Robert Grey, of Boston, having discovered the Columbia River in 1792, and named it after one of his vessels, the " Columbia ;" and the " Lewis and Clark Expedition " having in 1804–5 first explored the country from the Rocky Mountains to the Pacific Ocean. (2.) France having ceded this territory to Spain in 1762, and again obtained possession of it from Spain in 1800, three years previous to its purchase by the United States, the latter government, in consequence of an imperfect description of its boundaries in previous transfers, obtained from Spain, sixteen years later, a release of her claims to it, which release was incorporated into the treaty ceding Florida to the United States. (3.) Great Britain also claimed that part west of the Rocky Mountains, until the present boundary between the United States and the British Possessions was settled by treaty in 1846.

Territory ceded by Spain.—Florida, as ceded by Spain, embraced the territory within the present limits of that state, and all westward to the Mississippi River south of the 31st parallel, except the small area included within the Louisiana Purchase. Of this territory 2,300 square miles are now included within the State of Alabama, and 3,600 square miles within the State of Mississippi. By the same treaty Spain also ceded to the United States all claim to the territory embraced within the former Province of Louisiana.

Texas as Annexed.—The western boundary of Texas had not been settled at the time of her annexation, but she claimed as far westward as the Rio Grande, and northward to the Arkansas River. In 1850 her territory was reduced to its present limits by Congress, and in consideration of $10,000,000 she ceded to the United States all other territory to which she had any claim.

Territory ceded by Mexico in 1848.—The territory acquired from Mexico in 1848, by the "Treaty of Guadalupe Hidalgo," comprised all within the present limits of California, Nevada, and Utah, that part of Wyoming south of the 42d parallel and west of the Rocky Mountains, all of Colorado west of the dividing ridge of the Rocky Mountains and south of the Arkansas River, that part of New Mexico west of the Rio Grande and north of the Gila River, and all of Arizona north of the Gila River. Mexico also claimed the whole of Texas.

Territory ceded by Mexico in 1853.—Mexico ceded to the United States in 1853, by the "Gadsden Treaty," all that part of Arizona south of the Gila River, and that part of New Mexico west of the Rio Grande and south of the Gila River, and south of a direct line extending due west from the Rio Grande to the nearest branch of the Gila River.

3. SURFACE.

THE EASTERN PORTION.

The Atlantic Highland.—The Atlantic Highland is a broad but somewhat irregular belt of elevated country, 1,500 miles long, extending from the Gulf of St. Lawrence to Central Alabama, and conforming to the Atlantic coast in its general direction. It is surmounted by the Appalachian System of Mountains, consisting chiefly of a large number of narrow and nearly parallel ranges, with narrow valleys between them, known as the White Mountains in New Hampshire, the Green Mountains in Vermont, the Adirondac Mountains in northern New York, and by numerous local names further south, as the Alleghany Mountains in Virginia and North Carolina, and the Cumberland Mountains in Kentucky and Tennessee. These ranges have a general elevation of 2,000 to 3,000 feet. They are lowest in the central portion, and highest near their southern terminus, while some of their peaks are more than 6,000 feet high. Mt. Washington in New Hampshire, is the highest peak in the northern portion, having an elevation of 6,288 feet; and the Black Dome in North Carolina, is the highest in the southern portion, having an elevation of 6,707 feet.

A beautiful central valley extends through this system of mountains longitudinally, bordering Lake Champlain and the Hudson River in the north, and known as the Cumberland Valley in Pennsylvania, the Shenandoah Valley in Virginia, and further south as the Valley of East

Tennessee. In Pennsylvania this valley is hemmed in by mountains only in the west, the eastern ranges there disappearing below the surface.

The Appalachian Mountains have an average breadth of about 100 miles. They are bordered on the east by a section of hilly or rolling country, 20 to 100 miles in breadth, descending to the low plain of the Atlantic coast, and on the west by an undulating table-land, gently descending to the Mississippi Valley. They have three separate watersheds, or systems of drainage; (1.) by the streams flowing eastward and southward into the Atlantic; (2.) by those flowing westward into the Mississippi Basin; (3.) by those flowing westward and northward, into Lake Erie, Lake Ontario, and the St. Lawrence River. Their numerous streams furnish vast water-power facilities, which are extensively employed for manufacturing purposes. The Delaware, Susquehanna, and Potomac Rivers, have their sources in or near the western range and cut nearly through the entire belt, crossing its principal ranges transversely, while the Hudson River and its chief tributary, the Mohawk, cut entirely through.

The Atlantic Plain.—The Atlantic Plain, or Tide Water section, is a low flat belt, 20 to 100 miles in breadth, bordering the Atlantic coast, corresponding to the Cane-Brake section of the Gulf states. Its inland border is marked by a line of terraces, from which an intermediate belt rises to the foot of the mountains. Along the South Atlantic states this line also marks the navigable limits of the large streams, and the site of the chief inland cities. These cities, having tide-water connection, are favorably situated for utilizing the valuable water-power which the rivers everywhere afford at this line of terraces.

Basin of the Great Lakes.—This basin, while having

an outlet through the St. Lawrence River for a large accumulation of waters, receives the drainage of a comparatively small area on the south. The elevation of its southern rim, which separates it from the Mississippi Basin, is so slight that a canal, with no cutting more than 100 feet deep, would open an outlet to the waters of Lakes Superior, Michigan, Huron, and Erie, and change their course into the Mississippi River.

THE WESTERN PORTION.

The Pacific Highland.—The Pacific Highland, extending from the shores of the Arctic Ocean to the Isthmus of Panama, consists of a vast plateau, or succession of table-lands, surmounted by a great number of mountain ranges and lofty peaks, whose summits, in the more elevated regions, are covered with perpetual snow. The Rocky Mountains form its eastern limit, and the lofty Cascade and Sierra Nevada Range its western.

This plateau has a gradual but quite irregular increase in elevation from north to south, its general elevation being about 2,000 feet above the level of the sea in the Great Plains of the Columbia River, 3,000 to 4,000 feet in the valley of the Snake River, 4,250 feet in the Great Salt Lake Basin, Utah, 4,000 to 6,000 feet in Nevada, 5,000 to 7,000 feet in the basin drained by the Colorado River, and 8,000 feet at the base of the volcano Popocatapetl, in Mexico, where it attains its greatest altitude. Its general elevation and irregularities from east to west, in its broadest part, where it is crossed by the Pacific Railroad, will be seen from the altitude of some of the stations on the line of that road, showing the extremes of elevation and depression.

The altitude of Cheyenne is 6,041 feet; Sherman, 8,242

feet; Laramie, 7,123 feet; Fort Steele, 6,840 feet; Green River, 6,140 feet; Wahsatch, 6,879 feet; Ogden, 4,300 feet; Corinne, 4,229 feet; Promontory, 4,905 feet; Kelton, 4,222 feet; Pequop, 6,183 feet; Elko, 5,065 feet; Humboldt, 4,233 feet; White Plains, 3,893 feet; Reno, 4,507 feet; Truckee, 5,845 feet; Summit, 7,017 feet; Cisco, 5,939 feet; Blue Canyon, 4,677 feet; Colfax, 2,421 feet; Auburn, 1,362 feet; Sacramento, 30 feet. Thus it will be seen that from Cheyenne to Sherman there is an increase in elevation of 2,200 feet in a distance of 33 miles; while the descent from Summit to Sacramento, on the western slope of the Sierra Nevada Range, is almost 7,000 feet in a distance of 105 miles,—a change of climate from that of winter to summer, at certain seasons of the year, in less than half a day's travel.

The Rocky Mountains.—The Rocky Mountain System comprises a broad, irregular belt, having a breadth in some parts of 200 to 300 miles, extending from the Rio Grande River northward through western Texas, New Mexico, Colorado, Wyoming, Idaho, Montana, and beyond to the Arctic Ocean. Its main ranges are intersected by numerous cross-ranges, branches, and outlying spurs, and its culminating ridge forms the great water divide of the continent.

The Wind River Range, in the western part of Wyoming, is the most remarkable portion of this divide, sending its waters from nearly the same locality into three great rivers, which are the outlets of three widely separated and extensive systems of drainage. Dr. F. V. Hayden, United States Geologist, in his Report of 1873, referring to this locality, says: "There is perhaps no more unknown, nor more interesting geographical region in America than this great water divide of our continent. * * * Within a radius of ten miles may be found the sources of the three largest rivers in America. The general elevation is from 7,000 to 8,000 feet above the sea, while the mountains whose eternal snows form the sources of these great rivers, rise to a height of 10,000 to 12,000 feet. Flowing northward are the numerous branches of the Missouri, Yellowstone, and Wind Rivers, which all eventually unite into one mighty stream, the Missouri! To the south are the branches of the Green River, which unites with the Colorado, and finally empties into the Gulf of California; while south and west flow the branches of the Snake River, which, uniting with the Columbia, pour their vast volume of water into the Pacific."

Within the United States, the principal ranges of the Rocky Mountains have a mean elevation of about 10,000 feet, attaining their greatest altitude in Colorado, where the highest peaks are more than 14,000 feet above the level of the sea, and 6,000 to 8,000 feet higher than the surrounding country. Here the cross-ranges, which are chiefly of volcanic origin, cut up the longitudinal valleys into a succession of beautiful "parks," hemming them in on all sides by high mountain walls. The surrounding scenery is grand and delightful, while the parks are generally fertile, and many of them are already under cultivation.

The streams, everywhere throughout this vast mountain region, have cut out deep and almost impenetrable gorges or cañons, to the depth of hundreds, and often thousands of feet. In many places the erosive action has been enormous, disintegrating and carrying away immense masses of the mountains, leaving the harder portions standing up in lofty peaks, while the most wonderful columns, pinnacles, domes, castles, ampitheatres and other monumental and architectural forms, carved out by the same agents, are of frequent occurrence.

The mountain region of Colorado alone has an extent of nearly 70,000 square miles, or more than four times the entire area of Switzerland.

The Cascade and Sierra Nevada Mountains.—The Cascade Mountains in Washington Territory and Oregon, and the Sierra Nevada or "Snowy Range" in California, consist mainly of a continuous range, equal to the Rocky Mountains in height, and conforming in general direction to the Pacific coast, 120 to 180 miles distant. Between 35° and 40° north latitude its general elevation is 6,000 to 8,000 feet above the surrounding country, and it attains its greatest altitude in a cluster of lofty peaks, a few miles south of 37°. Mt. Whitney, in this cluster, is 15,000 feet high, and so far as known is the highest mountain in the United States. Mt. Shasta, near the north boundary of California, is 14,444 feet high, rising 7,000 feet higher than any other mountain within fifty miles; many other peaks in this range are 10,000 to 14,000 feet high.

These mountains have a narrow, abrupt slope to the plateaus on the east, and a broad slope, 50 to 70 miles in breadth, to the low valleys on the west. In the southern portion, near Mt. Whitney, the Sierra branches out into three separate ranges, between which lie the valleys of the two branches of Kern River. In the central portion it expands into a broad volcanic plateau, 200 miles long by 50 to 70 miles wide, extending from Warner's Range on the east to Mt. Shasta on the west.

From Mt. Shasta, branch ranges again lead away, uniting the Sierra with the comparatively low belt of mountains, 2,000 to 6,000 feet in height, and 20 to 50 miles in breadth, extending along the coast of California,

Oregon, and Washington Territory, known by the general name of "Coast Ranges."

The famous Yosemite Valley is situated in the western slope of the Sierra Nevada, in Mariposa County. It is a deep chasm, 8 miles long by half a mile to one mile wide, enclosed by granite walls, 3,000 to 5,000 feet high, over which the Merced River pours in beautiful cascades. One of these is an unbroken fall of more than 2,500 feet.

The Sacramento and San Joaquin Valley.—This valley, lying between the Sierra Nevada on the east, and the Coast Ranges on the west, is 400 miles long by about 50 miles broad. The northern portion is drained by the Sacramento, and the southern portion by the San Joaquin Rivers, which unite midway and break through the Coast Range to the Pacific. The surface is nearly level, having an elevation of 30 feet above the sea at the junction of these two rivers, and about 250 feet where they issue from the mountains. In the summer season most of the streams flowing eastward from the Coast Range are swallowed up in the sands before reaching their outlet into the Sacramento and San Joaquin Rivers, and the outlet to the Kern and Tulare Lakes also dries up.

The Willamette Valley.—A similar valley to that in California extends through the northern part of Oregon, and Washington Territory. In Oregon it is known as the Willamette Valley. It is separated from the Sacramento Valley of California by more than two hundred miles of mountainous country, in the northern portion of which is the comparatively small valley of the Umpaqua River, extending westward to the Pacific. The estimated area of this valley is 2,000 square miles, while the Willamette Valley has 8,000.

Deserts of California.—In the southeastern part of the

state is a large area of loose, shifting sand, about 140 miles long, by 50 to 70 miles wide, which is an arid desert, destitute of vegetation. Seventy-five miles northward, near the eastern boundary of the state, and within the Central Basin, is Death Valley, the sink of the Armagosa River. It is 30 miles long, 8 miles wide, and 150 feet below the level of the sea, and is totally dry except in the rainy season. It is one of the most desolate portions of that basin of deserts.

The Great Basin.—The vast region lying between the Wahsatch and Rocky Mountains on the east, and the Cascade and Sierra Nevada Mountains on the west, known as the "Great Basin," has an extent of nearly 1,000 miles from north to south, and 200 to 500 from east to west. It is much diversified by mountain ranges, interspersed with valleys, which sometimes expand into broad plains.

It is naturally divided into two separate basins, by an elevation extending along near the 42d parallel, forming the southern rim of the Basin of the Columbia River, and the northern rim of the Central Basin. On the southeast it is separated from the Basin of the Colorado River by the Wahsatch Mountains, a massive range nearly as high as the Rocky Mountains.

Basin of the Columbia River.—The mountain ranges in this basin generally lie in groups, each group connected together and radiating from a common nucleus, like the Salmon River Mountains, in Idaho, and the Blue Mountains, in Oregon. It is drained by the Columbia River and its tributaries. This basin contains extensive plains and valleys, among which are the Great Plains of the Columbia River, having an area of more than 20,000 square miles.

The Central Basin.—The Central Basin, embracing

western Utah, nearly all Nevada, and a small portion of California; is occupied by a large number of comparatively low, narrow, and mostly isolated ranges of mountains, having a general and very uniform north and south trend, with narrow valleys intervening. These mountains vary in elevation above the general surface of the plateau, from 1,000 to 6,000 feet.

There is no outlet for the drainage of this basin, nor is there any accumulation of waters within it, in excess of the annual amount carried off by evaporation. Many of its streams, fed by the melting snows in the mountains, dry up in the summer, and none add anything permanently to the volume of the lakes into which they flow. Nearly all of the lakes are salt or alkaline.

Great Salt Lake, which is 75 miles long, and covers an area of about 1,900 square miles, is much the largest salt lake in America, and the only lake of any considerable size within this basin. Its waters contain a fraction more than 20 per cent. of common salt, while their entire solid contents amount to less than $22\frac{1}{2}$ per cent. No fish is known to inhabit this lake, although Utah Lake, which is fresh, and has its outlet through the Jordan River into it, is well stocked with fish. Its elevation above the level of the sea is about 4,200 feet, and its principal sources of supply are the Bear, Weber, and Jordan Rivers, the first of which is more than 200 miles in length.

Basin of the Colorado River of the West.—The Colorado River of the West drains a large area, embracing within its limits the southwestern part of Wyoming, the eastern part of Utah, the western part of Colorado, and all of Arizona. In its lower portion, extending north from the head of the Gulf of California for a distance of nearly 300 miles, the general surface is low, nowhere rising more than a few hundred feet above the level of the sea, though here and there isolated ranges of mountains occur 2,000 to 6,000 feet high. This low part is hemmed in on the north by a line of bold and often nearly vertical cliffs, that rise hundreds or thousands of feet, to the table-lands, or plateaus above, 4,000 to 7,000 feet high, through which the river flows for many hundred miles.

These plateaus have a very uneven surface, and are dry and nearly destitute of vegetation at all seasons of the year, as is also the low portion of the basin. Maj. J. W. Powell says of this region:

"The principal condensation of moisture occurs on and about the mountains standing on the rim of the basin, the region within being arid. Bad-lands, alcove lands, plains of naked rock, plains of drifting sands, *mesas*, plateaus, buttes, hog-backs, cliffs, volcanic cones, volcanic mountains, cañons, cañon valleys, and valleys, are all found in this region and make up its topographical features. Mountains, hills, and small elevated valleys are features of the irregular boundary belt. * * *

"The Uinta Mountains were not thrust up as peaks, but were carved from a vast, rounded block, left by a retiring sea, or uplifted from the depths of the ocean, and its present forms are due to erosion. * * * The beds of sedimentary rocks on which these mountains stand, * * * at one time extended far away to the south, over this country and beyond the Grand Cañon. Shales, sandstones, and limestones, several thousand feet in thickness, have been washed away from the summit of all these benches. * * *

"All the mountain forms of this region are due to erosion; all the cañons, channels of living rivers and intermittent streams, were carved by the running waters, and they represent an amount of corrosion difficult to comprehend. But the carving of the cañons and mountains is insignificant, when compared with the denudation of the whole area, as evidenced in the cliffs of erosion. Beds, hundreds of feet in thickness, and hundreds of thousands of square miles in extent, beds of granite and beds of schist, beds of marble and beds of sandstone, crumbling shales and adamantine lavas, have slowly yielded to the silent and unseen powers of the air, and crumbled into dust, and been washed away by the rains and carried into the seas by the rivers."

THE MIDDLE PORTION.

The Mississippi Basin.—The Mississippi Basin, or Great Central Plain, as it is sometimes called, is a wide depression between the Appalachian Mountains on the east, and the Rocky Mountains on the west, drained by the Mississippi River and its vast number of tributaries.

This great basin consists of three principal slopes,—(1.) eastward, from the Rocky Mountains; (2.) westward, from the Appalachian Mountains; (3.) southward, from the Height of Land,—all leading to the central depression through which the Mississippi finds its way to the Gulf. These slopes are all gentle, as is shown by the small average descent of the principal streams that drain them; the descent of the Mississippi is less than eight inches per mile from its source to its mouth; that of the Ohio is five inches per mile from Pittsburgh to its mouth; that of the Missouri, from Fort Benton to its junction with the Mississippi, 381 feet above the level of the sea, is ten inches per mile. While at the base of the Rocky Mountains the general elevation is 5,000 to 6,000 above the sea, the descent of the Arkansas is but two feet per mile, and of the Red River but little more than one foot per mile.

Height of Land.—A broad swell of ground, called the "Height of Land," separates the Mississippi Basin from the basin of the Red River of the North. This elevation is 1,500 to 1,800 feet above the sea, abounding with lakes. Among them is Lake Itaska, the source of the Mississippi, at an elevation of 1,680 feet. The streams that rise here have their outlets in three separate and widely divergent systems of drainage: (1.) those flowing south into the Mississippi, having their outlet in the Gulf of Mexico; (2.) those flowing north into the Red River, having their outlet in Hudson's Bay; (3.) those flowing east into Lake Superior, having their outlet through the St. Lawrence River.

The lowest portion of the Mississippi Valley is a flat alluvial plain, 20 to 65 miles in breadth, through which the river flows from the mouth of the Ohio to the Gulf of Mexico. A nearly continuous line of bluffs extends along its border on either side, which frequently rise 150 to 200 feet high, forming an immense trough for the mighty stream, and setting bounds beyond which it cannot encroach. That this channel was excavated by the river, is evident from the corresponding layers of the stratified rocks, seen in the opposite bluffs. At one time it also formed an arm of the sea, through which the waters of the Gulf extended to the mouth of the Ohio. It has been filled up to its present level by sediment brought down by the river, the annual amount of which is estimated at more than forty million tons, or enough to build a pyramid a mile square at its base, 700 feet high.

This low country is sometimes called the "bottom lands," and portions of it are a nearly impenetrable swamp. Much of it is lower than the level of the river in time of high water, and is subject to frequent and wide-spread inundations. Extensive banks, or "levees," have been constructed to protect the surrounding country, but the water frequently breaks through and spreads over large districts. It is traversed by numerous "bayous" or lateral outlets, which are remnants of its main channel at some former time, or important divisions of it.

The amount of rainfall and moisture diminishes from the Mississippi River westward, until the well watered prairies gradually merge into a broad, arid belt, called the "Great Plains," totally unfit for tillage without irrigation. This dry belt is fully reached at about the one-hundredth meridian, extending westward to the Rocky Mountains, and from Mexico northward, along their eastern base to Arctic America.

IV. YELLOWSTONE NATIONAL PARK.

This tract was set apart by an Act of Congress, approved March 1, 1872, to be for ever reserved as a Public Park, or pleasure ground, bills with the necessary provisions having been introduced into both Houses of Congress in December, 1871,—in the Senate by Hon. S. C. Pomeroy, and in the House of Representatives by Hon. Wm. H. Claggett, delegate from Montana. The reservation comprises an area of 3,575 square miles, every part of which has an altitude of more than 6,000 feet, while its wonderful valleys are hemmed in on every side by lofty mountains, 10,000 to 12,000 feet high, covered with snow all the year round. During the summer months it has a pure and most invigorating atmosphere, and is nearly free from rain or storms of any kind; but no month is exempt from frosts. Within its limits are the Yellowstone Lake, Shoshone Lake, Madison Lake, the Upper and Lower Falls and the Grand Cañon of the Yellowstone River, hot springs without number, and the most wonderful geysers in the world.

Yellowstone Lake is situated at an altitude of 7,788 feet, and covers an area of 330 square miles. Dr. F. V. Hayden, United States Geologist, in his Report of 1872, describes it as "the most beautiful lake in the world, set like a gem among the mountains."

Falls and Grand Cañon of the Yellowstone.—Of the Falls and the Grand Cañon Dr. Hayden says: "It is only through the eye that the mind can gather anything like an adequate conception of them. As we approached the margin of the Cañon, we could hear the suppressed roar of the falls, resembling distant thunder. * * * Above the Upper Falls the Yellowstone flows through a grassy, meadow-like valley, in a calm, steady current, giving no warning until very near the falls that it is about to rush over a precipice 140 feet, and then within a quarter of a mile again to leap down a distance of 350 feet."

The river is 100 feet wide, and 30 feet deep, and in going over the falls it presents in the distance the appearance of a mass of snow-white foam. It is described as "a sight far more beautiful, though not so grand or impressive, as that of Niagara Falls." Dr. Hayden continues: Standing near the Lower Falls and looking down the cañon, * * * with its sides 1,200 to 1,500 feet high, and decorated with the most brilliant colors that the human eye ever saw, the rocks weathered into an almost unlimited variety of forms, with here and there a pine sending its roots into the clefts on the sides as if struggling with a sort of uncertain success to maintain an existence,—the whole presents a picture that it would be difficult to surpass in nature."

Erosive Forces.—In his report of 1873, Dr. Hayden

uses the following language respecting the erosion that has taken place here, and the beautiful scenery of these mountains:

"The erosive forces have cut deep cañons into the sides of the mountains, 2,500 to 3,000 feet through the conglomerates, and have worn the portions remaining into the most wonderful architectural forms. Domes, pyramids, pinnacles, palaces, indeed almost any form which one could conceive, can be seen here. One gorge was called the 'Palace Cañon,' on account of the symmetrical, palace-like forms which could be seen everywhere. The sides of these gorges are vertical walls, inaccessible, except in a few localities, to man or beast. One can stand in the bed of a little stream and look up the vertical walls on either side 2,500 or 3,000 feet. Such gorges as these, extending from five to twenty miles, oftentimes, are very numerous. Literally, hundreds of them may be found in these ranges, extending up to the very crest or water divide, carved out of the solid mass of conglomerate or trachyte. There is certainly no limit to the remarkable scenery which an artist could select in this prolific field."

Hot Springs.—The hot springs and geysers within the limits of the Yellowstone Park are said to number not less than ten thousand; yet, vast numbers that were once in an active state have since become extinct. In temperature many closely approach the boiling point, which at the various altitudes of these springs ranges from about 198° to 200° Fahrenheit. This region was formerly the center of great volcanic activity, the rocks being largely of volcanic origin, and these hot springs and geysers are the dying remnants of former volcanoes. The mineral deposits from the waters of these springs form around them in circular basins, which are frequently ornamented with the most beautiful bead-like incrustations, in great variety, and of the most exquisite colors. Some of them are thus described by the same writer: "We suddenly came in full view of one of the finest displays of nature's architectural skill the world can produce. * * * Before us was a hill 200 feet high, composed of the calcareous deposit of the hot springs, with a system of step-like terraces, which would defy any description by words. The eye alone can convey any adequate conception to the mind. The steep sides of the hill were ornamented with a series of semi-circular basins, with margins varying in height from a few inches to 6 or 8 feet, and so beautifully scalloped and adorned with a kind of bead-work that the beholder stands amazed at this marvel of nature's handiwork. Add to this a snow-white ground, with every variety of shade of scarlet, green, and yellow, as brilliant as the brightest of our aniline dyes. The pools or basins are of all sizes, from a few inches to 6 or 8 feet in diameter, and 2 inches to 2 feet deep. * * * The largest spring is very near the outer margin of the terraces, and is 25 by 40 feet in diameter, the water so perfectly transparent that one can look down into the ultramarine depth to the bottom of the basin. The sides of the basin are ornamented with coral-like forms, with a great variety of shades, from pure white to a bright cream yellow."

"On the north side of these hills, close to the foot, is a magnificent sulphur spring. The deposits around it are silica; but some places are white, and enameled like the finest porcelain. The thin edges of the nearly circular rim extend over the waters of the basin several feet, yet the open portion is 15 feet in diameter. The water is in a constant state of agitation. The stream that issues from this spring is so strong and hot that it was only on the windward side that I could approach it and ascertain its temperature, 197°. The agitation seemed to affect the entire mass, carrying it up impulsively to the height of 4 feet. It may be compared to a huge cauldron of perfectly clear water somewhat superheated. But it is the decorations about this spring that lent the charm, after our astonishment at the seething mass before us—the most beautiful scalloping around the rim, and the inner and outer surface covered with a pearl-like bead-work. * * * No kind of embroidering that human art can conceive or fashion could equal this specimen of the cunning skill of nature."

Fire Hole Valley.—This valley, in which most of these springs are situated, is about 20 miles long by 5 miles wide, and its appearance is thus described: " Early in the morning of August 30, the valley was literally filled with columns of steam, ascending from more than a thousand vents. I can compare the view to nothing but that of some manufacturing city, like Pittsburgh, as seen from a high point, except that instead of the black coal smoke, there are here the white delicate clouds of steam."

Mud Springs.—There are also hundreds of mud springs, or " mud volcanoes," as they are sometimes called, having basins varying from a few feet to seventy-five feet, or more, in diameter, and their contents are of all degrees of consistency, from mere turbid water to thick mortar.

Some of these springs on Cascade Creek, are thus described:

"The first one is a remarkable mud spring, with a well-defined circular rim, composed of fine clay, and raised about 4 feet above the surface around, and about 6 feet above the mud in the basin. The diameter of the basin is about 8 feet. The mud is so fine as to be impalpable, and the whole may be compared to a caldron of boiling mush. * * * This mud, which has been wrought in these caldrons for perhaps hundreds of years, is so fine and pure that the manufacturer of porcelain ware would go into ecstacy at the sight. The contents of many of the springs are of such a snowy whiteness that when dried in cakes in the sun or by a fire, they resemble the finest meerschaum. * * * Not far from the grotto, is the most remarkable mud spring we have ever seen in the West. The rim of the basin is formed of the loose mud or clay thrown out of the orifice. It is about 40 feet in diameter at the top, but tapering down to half the size, and is about 30 feet deep. It may not improperly be called the 'Giants' Caldron.' It does not boil with an impulse like most of the mud springs, but with a constant roar, which shakes the ground for a considerable distance, and may be heard for half a mile. A dense column of steam is ever rising, filling the crater, but now and then a passing breeze will remove it for a moment, revealing one of the most terrific sights one could well imagine."

Geysers.—Great numbers of geysers exist, varying in size from small jets to huge columns of water many feet in diameter, thrown out with an immense force, at frequent, but generally quite irregular intervals. One, not less than 20 feet in diameter, has been observed to throw a column of water 60 feet high. Another throws a column 6 feet in diameter 140 to 200 feet high. Another throws a column 5 or 6 feet in diameter 200 feet high, while smaller streams are sometimes thrown as high as 250 feet. Very interesting descriptions of many of these remarkable geysers are also given by Dr. Hayden, from which the following brief extracts are taken.

"We camped on the evening of August 5th, in the middle of the Upper Geyser Basin, in the midst of some of the grandest geysers in the world. Col. Barlow and Capt. Heap, of the United States Engineers, were camped on the opposite side of the Fire Hole. Soon after reaching camp a tremendous rumbling was heard, shaking the ground in every direction, and soon a column of steam burst forth from a crater near the edge of the east side of the river. Following the steam, arose, by a succession of impulses, a column of water apparently 6 feet in diameter, to the height of two hundred feet, while the steam ascended a thousand feet or more. * * * We called this Grand Geyser. * * * It is a very modest looking spring in a state of quiescence, and no one would for a moment suspect the power that was temporarily slumbering below. * * * Within 20 feet of this orifice is a second one, of irregular, quadrangular form, 15 by 25 feet. * * * The large orifice seems to be in a state of violent agitation as often as once in 20 minutes, raising up the entire mass of water 10 or 15 feet. It is never altogether quiet. Although these two orifices are within the same rim, I could not ascertain that there is the slightest connection between them. * * * The Grand Geyser operated twice while we were in the basin, with an interval of about 32 hours."

"Just east of the Grand Geyser is a moderate sized geyser, with three smaller ones along side of it, all playing at the same time. From the large one a column of water is constantly shot up 15 or 20 feet, with much the sound of the escape of steam from a pipe. The orifice is not more than 6 inches in diameter, but with the three smaller ones playing at the same time a great commotion is excited."

"The Giant has a crater like a broken horn, 5 or 6 feet in diameter, and while my party were in the basin, played at one time one hour and twenty minutes, throwing the water up to the height of 140 feet."

"Our search for new wonders leading us across the Fire Hole River, we ascended a gentle incrusted slope, and came suddenly upon a large oval aperture with scalloped edges, the diameters of which were 18 and 25 feet, the sides corrugated and covered with a grayish-white siliceous deposit, which was distinctly visible at the depth of 100 feet below the surface. No water could be discovered, but we could distinctly hear it gurgling and boiling at a great distance below. Suddenly it began to rise, boiling and spluttering, and sending out huge masses of steam, causing a general stampede of our company, driving us to some distance from our point of observation. When within about 40 feet of the surface it became stationary, and we returned to look down upon it. All at once it seemed seized with a fearful spasm and rose with incredible rapidity, hardly affording us time to flee to a safe distance, when it burst from the orifice with terrible momentum, rising in a column the full size of this immense aperture to the height of 60 feet; and through and out of the apex of this vast aqueous mass, five or six lesser jets or round columns of water, varying from 6 to 15 inches in diameter, were projected to the marvelous height of 250 feet. * * * This grand eruption continued for twenty minutes, and was the most magnificent sight we ever witnessed. Two of these wonderful eruptions occurred during the twenty-two hours we remained in the valley. This geyser we named 'The Giantess.'

"A hundred yards distant from the Giantess was a siliceous cone, very symmetrical, * * three feet in height and 5 feet in diameter at its base, having an oval orifice 24 by 36 inches in diameter, with scalloped edges. Not one of our company supposed that it was a geyser; and among so many wonders it had almost escaped notice. While we were at breakfast upon the morning of our departure, a column of water entirely filling the crater shot from it, which, by accurate triangular measurement we found to be 219 feet in height. * * We named it the 'Beehive.' The Fan Geyser consists of a group of five geysers which play at one time, throwing the water in every direction."

" As we were leaving the valley, the grand old geyser which stands sentinel at the head of the valley gave us a magnificent parting display, and with little or no preliminary warning it shot up a column of water about six feet in diameter to the height of 100 to 150 feet, and by a succession of impulses seemed to hold it up steadily for the space of fifteen minutes. * * * On account of its apparent regularity, and its position overlooking the valley, it was called by Messrs. Langford and Doane 'Old Faithful.'

" We left this valley with its beautiful scenery, its hot springs and geysers, with great regret."

V. CANONS OF THE COLORADO RIVER OF THE WEST.

The Colorado River of the West, for more than a thousand miles, flows through an immense gorge, or a succession of vast cañons, cut down through the solid rocks to a surprising depth by the action of its waters. These rocks stand up on either side in grand and awful precipices,— sometimes in nearly vertical walls, or overhanging cliffs, thousands of feet high. The depth of the gorge is seldom less than 2,000 feet, often increasing to 3,000, or more, and sometimes to 5,000 or 6,000 feet, the river, in the deepest cañon being more than one mile below the surface of the surrounding country.

Major J. W. Powell, who has spent several years in exploring the cañons of this remarkable river and its tributaries, uses the following language in speaking of its sources and the region through which it flows:

"The Colorado River is formed by the junction of the Grand and Green. The Grand river has its source in the Rocky Mountains, five or six miles west of Long's Peak. * * * The Green River heads near Frémont's Peak, in the Wind River Mountains. * * * This river, like the last, has its sources in alpine lakes, fed by everlasting snows."

"The Green River is larger than the Grand, and is the upper continuation of the Colorado. Including this river, the whole length of the stream is about 2,000 miles. The region of country drained by the Colorado and its tributaries is about 800 miles in length, and varies from 300 to 500 in width, containing about 300,000 square miles."

"The upper two-thirds of the basin rises from four to eight thousand feet above the level of the sea. This high region, on the east, north, and west, is set with ranges of snow-clad mountains, attaining an altitude above the sea varying from 8,000 to 14,000 feet. All winter long, on its mountain-crested rim, snow falls, filling the gorges, half burying the forests, and covering the crags and peaks with a mantle woven by the winds from the waves of the sea—a mantle of snow. When the summer-sun comes, this snow melts and tumbles down the mountain sides in millions of cascades. Ten million cascade brooks unite to form ten thousand torrent creeks; ten thousand torrent creeks unite to form a hundred rivers beset with cataracts; a hundred roaring rivers unite to form the Colorado, which rolls, a mad, turbid stream, into the Gulf of California."

"Now, if at the river's flood, storms were falling on the plains, its channel would be cut but little faster than the adjacent country would be washed, and the general level would thus be preserved; but under the conditions here mentioned the river deepens its bed, as there is much through corrosion and but little lateral degradation. So all the streams cut deeper and still deeper until their banks are towering cliffs of solid rock. These deep, narrow gorges are called cañons. For more than a thousand miles along its course, the Colorado has cut for itself such a cañon; but at some few points, where lateral streams join it, the cañon is broken, and narrow, transverse valleys divide it properly into a series of cañons."

"Every river entering these has cut another cañon; every lateral creek has cut a cañon; every brook runs in a cañon; every rill born of a shower, and born again of a shower, and living only during these showers, has cut for itself a cañon; so that the whole upper portion of the basin of the Colorado is traversed by a labyrinth of these deep gorges."

Major Powell, starting from Green River City with ten men in boats, descended the Green River to its junction with the Grand, and the Colorado to the mouth of the Virgin River, passing through the most stupendous series of river cañons on the face of the globe. A few extracts from that gentleman's very interesting and graphic report of his perilous voyage, will convey some idea of the magnitude and grandeur of those cañons.

"May 26. We pass down to the foot of the Uinta Mountains, and in a cold storm go into camp. The river is running to the south; the mountains have an easterly and westerly trend directly athwart its course, yet it glides on in a quiet way, as if it thought a mountain range no formidable obstruction to its course. It enters the range by a flaming, brilliant, red gorge, that may be seen from the north a score of miles away. The great mass of the mountain-ridge through which the gorge is cut, is composed of bright vermilion rocks. * * * This is the head of the first cañon we are about to explore—an introductory one to a series made by the river through this range. We name it Flaming Gorge. The cliffs or walls we find, on measurement, to be about one thousand two hundred feet high. * * * The distance from Green River City to Flaming Gorge is sixty-two miles."

"Entering Flaming Gorge we quickly run through it on a swift current, and emerge into a little park. Half a mile below, the river wheels sharply to the left, and we turn into another cañon cut into the mountain. We enter the narrow passage. On either side the walls rapidly increase in altitude. On the left are overhanging cliffs five hundred—a thousand—fifteen hundred feet high. On the right the rocks are broken and ragged, and the water fills the channel from cliff to cliff. Now the river turns abruptly around a point to the right, and the waters plunge swiftly down among great rocks; and here we have our first experience with cañon rapids. * * * Soon our boats reach the swift current; a stroke or two, now on this side, now on that, and we thread the narrow passage with exhilarating velocity, mounting the high waves, whose foaming crests dash over us, and plunging into the troughs, until we reach the quiet water below; and then comes a feeling of great relief. Our first rapid is run."

A LANDSCAPE OF NAKED ROCK.

"July 8. This morning Bradley and I go out to climb, and gain an altitude of more than 2,000 feet above the river, but still do not reach the summit of the wall. After dinner we pass through a region of the wildest desolation. The cañon is very tortuous, the river very rapid, and many lateral cañons enter on either side. In several places these lateral cañons are only separated from each other by narrow walls, often hundreds of feet high, but so narrow in places that where softer rocks are found below they have crumbled away, and left holes in the wall, forming passages from one cañon into another."

"In many places the walls, which rise from the water's edge, are overhanging on either side. The stream is still quiet, and we glide along through a strange, weird, grand region. The landscape everywhere, away from the river, is of rock—cliffs of rock, tables of rock, plateaus of rock, crags of rock—ten thousand strangely carved forms. Rocks everywhere, and no vegetation, no soil, no sand. In long, gentle curves, the river winds about these rocks."

"When speaking of these rocks we must not conceive of piles of boulders, or heaps of fragments, but a whole land of naked rock, with giant forms carved on it; cathedral shaped buttes, towering hundreds or thousands of feet; cliffs that cannot be scaled, and cañon walls that shrink the river into insignificance, with vast, hollow domes, and tall pinnacles, and shafts set on the verge overhead, and all highly colored—buff, gray, red, brown, and chocolate—never lichened, never moss-covered, but bare, and often polished. * * * Late in the afternoon the water becomes swift, and our boats make great speed. An hour of this rapid running brings us to the junction of the Grand and Green, the foot of Stillwater Cañon, as we have named it."

"The Cañon of Desolation is 97 miles long : Gray Cañon, 36; Labyrinth Cañon, 62½ miles. In the Cañon of Desolation the highest rocks immediately over the river are about 2,400 feet. * * * Climbing the walls of the Cañon and passing back to the cañon terrace and climbing that, we find the altitude above the river to be 3,300 feet. The lower end of Gray Cañon is about 2,000 feet high, and the lower end of Labyrinth Cañon 1,300 feet. Stillwater Cañon is 42¾ miles long; the highest walls 1,300 feet."

"July 21. We start this morning on the Colorado. The river is rough, and bad rapids, in close succession are found. Two very hard portages are made during the forenoon. After dinner, in running a rapid, the 'Emma Dean' is swamped, and we are thrown into the river; we cling to her, and in the first quiet water below she is righted and bailed out, but three oars are lost."

"Aug. 9. Now the scenery is on a grand scale. The walls of the cañon, 2,500 feet high, are of marble, of many beautiful colors, and often polished below by the waves, or far up the sides, where showers have washed the sands over the cliff. At one place I have a walk for more than a mile on a marble pavement, all polished and fretted with strange devices, and embossed in a thousand fantastic patterns."

"Aug. 13. We are three-quarters of a mile in the depths of the earth, and the great river shrinks into insignificance as it dashes its angry waves against the walls and cliffs that rise to the world above; they are but puny ripples, and we but pigmies, running up and down the sands."

"Aug. 14. The walls now are more than a mile in height—a vertical distance difficult to appreciate. * * * A thousand feet of this is up through granite crags, then steep slopes and perpendicular cliffs rise, one above another to the summit. The gorge is black and narrow below, red and gray and flaring above, with crags and angular projections on the walls, which, cut in many places by side cañons seem to be a wilderness of rocks. Down in these grand, gloomy depths we glide, ever listening, for the mad waters keep up their roar; ever watching, ever peering ahead, for the narrow cañon is winding, and the river is closed in so that we can see but a few hundred yards, and what there may be below we know not; but we listen for falls, and watch for rocks, or stop now and then in a bay or recess, to admire the gigantic scenery."

"Aug. 25. Great quantities of cooled lava, and many cinder cones are seen on either side. * * * On the right wall, a cinder cone, or extinct volcano, with a well-defined crater, stands on the very brink of the cañon. From this volcano vast floods of lava have been poured down into the river, and a stream of molten rock has run up the cañon three or four miles, and down, we know not how far. * * * The cañon was doubtless filled to a height of twelve or fifteen hundred feet, perhaps by more than one flood. This would dam the water back; and in cutting through this great lava bed a new channel has been formed, sometimes on one side, sometimes on the other. * * * What a conflict of water and fire there must have been here! Just imagine a river of molten rock, running down into a river of melted snow. What a seething and boiling of the waters; what clouds of steam rolled into the heavens!"

"Aug. 29. We start very early this morning. The river still continues swift, but we have no serious difficulty, and at 12 o'clock emerge from the Grand Cañon of the Colorado."

On the following day the expedition arrived at the mouth of the Virgin River, 60 or 70 miles below the Grand Cañon. The Grand Cañon is 217 miles long, and its greatest depth is 6,200 feet. Major Powell, referring to some of the impressions which these great depths produced, and the appearance of this wonderful chasm, says: "The varying depths of this cañon, due to the varying altitudes of the plateaus through which it runs, can only be seen from above. As we wind about in the gloomy depths below, the difference between 4,000 and 6,000 feet is not discerned. * * In the very depths of the cañon we have black granite, with a narrow cleft, through which a great river plunges. This granite portion of the walls is carved with deep gulches, and embossed with pinnacles and towers. Above, are broken, ragged, non-conformable rocks, in many places sloping back at a low angle. Clambering over these, we reach rocks lying in horizontal beds. Some are soft, many very hard; the softer strata are washed out; the harder remain as shelves. Everywhere there are side gulches and cañons, so that these gulches are set above with ten thousand dark, gloomy alcoves. One might imagine that this was intended for the library of the gods—and it was. The shelves are not for books, but form the stony leaves of one great book. He who would read the language of the universe, may dig out letters here and there, and with them spell the words, and read, in a slow and imperfect way, but so as to understand a little, the story of creation."

V. ANCIENT LAKE BASINS.

Ample evidences exist, that large portions of the vast area, extending from western Nebraska to the Pacific Ocean, were once occupied by great fresh-water lakes;

and no more interesting evidence of the wonderful changes that have taken place on this continent, as regards both surface and climate, can be found, than the records which these old lake basins furnish. Dr. F. V. Hayden, United States Geologist, uses the following language respecting one of these basins, principally occupying western Utah and Nevada:

"It is most probable that at a comparatively modern period the vast area between the Wahsatch Mountains on the east, and the Sierra Nevada on the west, was one great lake, the mountains rising up like islands in this vast inland sea. The lakes, large and small, which we find scattered over the basin at the present time, are only remnants of this former sea. The modern deposits which cover the low lands are mostly calcareous and arenaceous beds, and sometimes reach a thickness of 800 to 1,200 feet, often filled with fresh water or land shells, indicating a very modern origin."

Among many other old lake basins referred to by Dr. Hayden, are two important ones in western Nebraska and southern Dakota:

"We now pass the eastern shore of one of the most interesting and most wonderful of those great lake basins which are found all over the west, from the Missouri River to the Pacific coast. There is no water in it at the present time, and its existence is only known to the student of geology. During the tertiary period it occupied an area of at least one hundred thousand, and very possibly of one hundred and fifty thousand, square miles. It will thus be seen that our greatest northern lakes, of which we so proudly boast, are but ponds in comparison with some that existed in this mountain region."

"The valleys of Loup Fork and the Niobrara Rivers,

although largely uninhabitable, are full of interest to the geologist. Located along these rivers is one of those grand cemeteries of extinct animals, which have excited the wonder of intelligent men all over the world. Further to the northwest, on White Earth River, is another of these far-famed bone deposits. These two interesting localities bear such a relation to each other in the order of time, and the relationship of the animals preserved in them, that they should be described in the same connection. I will therefore take the reader at once to the valley of White Earth River, near the south-western base of the Black Hills, and there we shall behold one of the wildest regions on this continent. It has always gone by the name of 'bad lands;' by the Canadian French, '*Mauvaises Terres;*' in the Dakota tongue, '*Ma-Koó-si-tcha.*' These words signify a very difficult country to travel through, not only from the ruggedness of the surface, but also from the absence of any good water, and the small supply of wood and game. * * It is only to the geologist that this place can have any permanent attractions. He can wind his way through the wonderful cañons among some of the grandest ruins in the world. Indeed, it resembles a gigantic city fallen to decay. Domes, towers, minarets, and spires may be seen on every side, which assume a great variety of shapes when viewed in the distance. Not unfrequently the rising or setting sun will light up these grand old ruins with a wild, strange beauty, reminding one of a city illuminated in the night from some high point. The harder layers project from the sides of the valley or cañon with such regularity that they appear like seats, one above the other, of some vast ampitheater. It is at the foot of these apparent architectural ruins that the curious fossil treasures are found. In the oldest beds

ANCIENT LAKE BASINS. 41

we find the teeth and jaws of a Hyopotamus, a river horse much like the Hippopotamus, which must have sported in his pride in the marshes that bordered this lake. So, too, the Titanotherium, a gigantic pachyderm, was associated with a species of hornless Rhinoceros. These huge rhinoceroid animals appear at first to have monopolized this entire region, and the plastic, sticky clay of the lowest bed of this basin, in which the remains were found, seems to have formed a suitable bottom of the lake in which these thick-skinned monsters could wallow at pleasure. As we pass higher up in the sediments we find the remains of a great variety of land animals, mingled with those that were aquatic in their nature. In a bed of flesh-colored marl, which is visible for a great distance, like a broad band in the sides of these washed hills, thousands of turtles were imbedded, and are preserved to the present time with surprising perfection, the hard portions being as complete as when they were swimming about in these tertiary waters hundreds of thousands of years ago. They vary in size from an inch or two in length across the back, to three or four feet."

"If we pass for a moment southward into the valleys of the Niobrara and Loup Fork, we shall find a fauna closely allied, yet entirely distinct from the one on White River, and plainly intermediate between that of the latter and of the present period ; one appears to have lived during the middle or miocene tertiary period, and the other at a later time, in what is called the pliocene. In the later fauna were the remains of a number of species of extinct camels, one of which was of the size of the Arabian camel, a second about two-thirds as large, also a smaller one. The only animals akin to the camels at the present time in the western hemisphere, are the Llama and its allies in South America. Not less interesting are the remains of a great variety of forms of the horse family, one of which was about as large as the ordinary domestic animal, and the smallest not more than two or two and a half feet in height, with every intermediate grade in size."

"There was still another animal allied to the horse, about the size of a Newfoundland dog, which was provided with three hoofs to each foot, though the lateral hoofs were rudimental. Although no horses were known to exist on this continent prior to its discovery by Europeans, yet Dr. Leidy has shown that before the age of man, this was emphatically the country of horses. Dr. Leidy has reported twenty-seven species of the horse family which are known to have lived on this continent prior to the advent of man—about three times as many as are now found living throughout the world."

"Five species of the Rhinoceros roamed through these marshes, ranging from a small, hornless species, about the size of our black bear, to the largest, which was about the size of the existing unicorn of India. No animals of the kind now inhabit the western hemisphere. Among the thick-skinned animals were the remains of a mastodon, and a large elephant, distinct from any others heretofore discovered in any part of the world. During the tertiary period Nebraska and Dakota were the homes of a race of animals closely allied to those inhabiting Asia and Africa now, and from their character we may suppose that during that period the climate was considerably warmer than it is at present. The inference is also drawn that our world, which is usually called the new, is in reality the old world, older than the eastern hemisphere."

The following extracts are from an interesting chapter

on "The Ancient Lakes of Western America," by Dr. J. S. Newberry:

"The wonderful collections of fossil plants and animal remains brought by Dr. Hayden from the country bordering the Upper Missouri have been shown, by his observations and the researches of Mr. Meek, to have been derived from deposits made in extensive fresh-water lakes—lakes which once occupied much of the region lying immediately east of the Rocky Mountains, but which have now totally disappeared. The sediments that accumulated in the bottoms of these old lakes show that·in the earliest periods of their history they contained salt water, at least that the sea had access to them, and their waters were more or less impregnated with salt, so as to be inhabited by oyster and other marine or estuary mollusks. In due time the continental elevation which brought all the country west of the Mississippi up out of the wide-spread cretaceous sea, raised these lake basins altogether above the sea level, and surrounded them with a broad expanse of dry land. Then ensued one of the most interesting chapters in the geological history of our continent, and one that, if fairly written out, could not fail to be read with pleasure by all intelligent persons."

"It has happened to me to be connected with three of the Government surveys to which I have referred, and to spend several years in traversing the great area lying between the Columbia River and the Gulf of Mexico. The observations which I have made on the geological structure of our western territories supplement, in a somewhat remarkable way, those made by Dr. Hayden, so that, taken together, our reports embody the results of a reconnoissance stretching over nearly the whole of our vast possessions west of the Mississippi."

"Parallel with the Coast Mountains lies a narrow trough, which, in California is traversed by the Sacramento and San Joaquin Rivers, and portions of it have received their names. Further north this trough is partially filled, and for some distance nearly obliterated by encroachment of the neighboring mountain ranges, but in Oregon and Washington it reappears essentially the same in structure as further south, and is here traversed by the Willamette and Cowlitz Rivers."

"These two sections of this great valley have now free drainage to the Pacific, through the Golden Gate and the trough of the Columbia, both of which are channels cut by the drainage water through mountain barriers that formerly obstructed its flow, and produced an accumulation behind them that made these valleys inland lakes—the first of the series I am to describe of extensive fresh-water basins that formerly gave character to the surface of our Western Territory, and that have now almost all been drained away and disappeared."

"East of the California Valley, the Sierra Nevada lies, like a lofty mountain chain, reaching all the way from our northern to our southern boundary."

"The crest of the Sierra Nevada is so high and continuous that for one thousand miles it shows no passes less than five thousand feet above the sea, and yet at three points there are gateways opened in this wall, by which it may be passed but little above the sea level. These are the cañons of the Sacramento, (Pit River,) the Klamath, and the Columbia. All these are gorges cut through this great dam by the drainage of the continent. In the lapse of ages the cutting down of this barrier has progressed to such an extent as almost completely to empty the great

ANCIENT LAKE BASINS.   45

water basins that once existed behind it, and leave the interior the arid waste that it is."

"The northern part of this area is drained by the Columbia; the southern by the Colorado. Of these the Columbia makes its way into the ocean by the gorge it has cut in the Cascade Mountains, through which it flows nearly at the sea level; while the Colorado flows to the Gulf of California through a series of cañons, of which the most important is nearly one thousand miles in length, and from three thousand to six thousand feet in depth. In volume 6 of the Pacific Railroad Reports, I have described a portion of the country drained by the Columbia, and have given the facts that lead me to assert that the gorge through which it passes the Cascade Mountains has been excavated by its waters; and that previous to the cutting down of this barrier these waters accumulated to form great freshwater lakes, which left deposits at an elevation of more than two thousand feet above the present bed of the Columbia. Similar facts were observed in the country drained by the Klamath and Pit Rivers."

"The animal remains contained in these fresh-water deposits * * consist of bones of the mastodon, rhinoceros, horse, elk, and other large mammals, which the species are probably in some cases new, in others identical with those obtained from the fresh-water tertiaries of the 'bad lands' by Dr. Hayden. With these mammalian remains are a few bones of birds and great numbers of the bones and teeth of fishes. * * There are also in this collection large numbers of fresh-water shells."

"All these fossils show that at one period in the history of our continent, and that, geologically speaking, quite recent, the region under consideration was thickly set with lakes, some of which were of larger size and greater depth than the great fresh-water lakes which now lie upon our northern frontier. Between these lakes were areas of dry land covered with a luxuriant and beautiful vegetation, and inhabited by herds of elephants and other great mammals, such as could only inhabit a well-watered and fertile country. In the streams flowing into these lakes, and in the lakes themselves, were great numbers of fishes and mollusks of species which, like the others I have enumerated, have now disappeared. At that time, as now, the great lakes formed evaporating surfaces, which produced showers that vivified all their shores. Every year, however, saw something removed from the barriers over which their surplus waters flowed to the sea, and, in the lapse of time they were drained to the dregs. In the Klamath Lakes, and in San Francisco, San Pablo and Suisun Bays, we have the last remnants of these great bodies of water; while the drainage of the Columbia lakes has been so complete, that in some instances the streams which traverse their old basins have cut two thousand feet into the sediments which accumulated beneath their waters."

" The history of this old lake country, as it is recorded in the alternations of strata which accumulated at the bottoms of its water basins, will be found to be full of interest. For while these strata furnish evidence that there were long intervals when peace and quiet prevailed over this region, and animal and vegetable life flourished as they now do nowhere on the continent, they also prove that this quiet was at times disturbed by the most violent volcanic eruptions from a number of distinct centers of action, but especially from the great craters which crowned the summit of the Sierra Nevada. From these came showers of ashes which must have covered the land and filled the water so as to destroy immense numbers of the inhabitants of both. These ashes formed strata which were in some instances ten or twenty feet in thickness.

"At other times the volcanic action was still more intense, and floods of lava were poured out, which formed continuous sheets hundreds of miles in extent, penetrating far into the lake basins, and giving to their bottoms floors of solid basalt. When these cataclysms had passed, quiet was again restored, forests again covered the land, herds dotted its pastures, fishes peopled the waters, and fine sediments abounding in forms of life accumulated in new sheets above the strata of cooled lava. The banks of the Des Chutes and Columbia Rivers afford splendid sections of these lava deposits, where the history I have so hastily sketched may be read as from an open book."

"But it will be said that there are portions of the great central plateau which have not been drained in the manner I have described. For here are basins which have no outlets, and which still hold sheets of water of greater or less area, such as those of Pyramid Lake, Salt Lake, &c. The history of these basins is very different from that of those already mentioned, and not less interesting or easily read. By the complete drainage of the northern and southern thirds of the plateau through the channels of the Columbia and Colorado, the water surface of this great area was reduced to the tenth or hundredth part of the space it previously occupied. Hence the moisture suspended in the atmosphere was diminished in like degree, and the dry, hot air, sweeping over the plains, licked up the water from the undrained lakes until they were reduced to their present dimensions. Now, as formerly, they receive the constant flow of the streams that drain into them from the mountains on the east and west. But the evaporation is so rapid that their dimensions are not only not increased thereby, but are steadily diminishing from year to year."

"On the east of the Rocky Mountains lies the country of the 'Plains,' a region not unlike in its topography to the great plateau of the West, but differing in this, that it is not bordered on the east by a continuous mountain chain; that it slopes gently downward to the Mississippi, and that its eastern half has been so well watered that its valleys have been made broad, and all its topographical features softened down. In former times, however, the topographical unity now conspicuous on the Plains did not exist, and the surface was marked by a series of great basins, which received the flow of water from the Rocky Mountains and formed lakes, less numerous, it is true, but of greater extent than those of the far West."

"The number of fossil plants and animals is much greater there than further west; and we have in these deposits proof that during unnumbered ages, this portion of the continent exhibited a diversified and beautiful surface, which sustained a luxuriant growth of vegetation and an amount of animal life, far in excess of what it has done in modern times. This condition of things existed long enough for hundreds and even thousands of feet of sediments to accumulate in the bottoms of these fresh-water lakes, which were gradually and slowly diminished in area by the filling up of their basins and by the wearing away of the barriers over which passed their gently flowing, draining streams."

"In the beginning of the cretaceous age, North America presented a broad land surface, having a climate similar to the present, and covered with forests, consisting for the most part of trees belonging to the same genera with those that now flourish upon it. In the progress of the cretaceous age, the greater part of the continent west of the Mississippi sank beneath the ocean, and the deposits made during the later portions of the cretaceous age contain a vegetation more tropical in character than that which had preceded it. It seems probable that at this time the lands which existed as such west of the Mississippi were islands of limited extent, washed by the Gulf Stream, which apparently had then a course north and west from the Gulf of Mexico to the Arctic Sea. The earlier tertiary epochs were, however, marked by an emergence of the continent, and a gradual approach to previous and present conditions."

"The climate of the continent in the miocene age was much milder than now. Fan-palms then grew as far north as the Yellowstone River, and a flora flourished in Alaska and Greenland as varied and as luxuriant as now grows along the fortieth parallel. * * This state of things seems to have continued through the pliocene age, and up to the time when the climate of the continent was completely revolutionized by the advent of the ice period. The change which took place at that time was such as taxes the imagination to conceive of as much as it taxes the reasoning powers to account for."

"We have seen that in the middle tertiary age the climate of Alaska and Greenland was that of New York and St. Louis at present. In the next succeeding period, the glacial epoch, the present climate of Greenland was brought down to New York, and all the northern portion of the continent wrapped in ice and snow. This change was undoubtedly gradual, (for nature does not often 'turn a corner,') but it is plain that it must have resulted in the gradual driving southward of all the varied forms of animal and vegetable life that spread over the continent to

4

the Arctic Sea. When glaciers reached as far south as the fortieth parallel it is evident that a cold, temperate climate prevailed in Mexico, and that only in the south of Mexico would the average annual temperature have been what it was previously in the latitude of New York. We must conclude, therefore, that the herds of mammals which once covered the plains of the interior of North America were forced by the advancing cold into such narrow limits in Southern Mexico that nearly all were exterminated."

"The pictures which geology holds up to our view of North America during the tertiary ages, are in all respects, but one, more attractive and interesting than could be drawn from its present aspects. Then a warm and genial climate prevailed from the Gulf to the Arctic Sea; the Canadian highlands were higher, but the Rocky Mountains lower and less broad. Most of the continent exhibited an undulating surface, rounded hills and broad valleys covered with forests grander than any of the present day, or wide expanses of rich savannah, over which roamed countless herds of animals, many of gigantic size, of which our present meager fauna retains but a few dwarfed representatives. Noble rivers flowed through plains and valleys, and sea-like lakes, broader and more numerous than those the continent now bears, diversified the scenery. Through unnumbered ages the seasons ran their ceaseless course, the sun rose and set, moons waxed and waned over this fair land, but no human eye was there to mark its beauty, nor human intellect to control and use its exuberant fertility. Flowers opened their many-colored petals on meadow and hillside, and filled the air with their perfumes, but only for the delectation of the wandering bee. Fruits ripened in the sun, but there was no hand to pluck, nor any speaking tongue to taste. Birds sang in the trees, but for no ears but their own. The surface of lake or river was whitened by no sail, or furrowed by no prow but the breast of the water-fowl; and the far-reaching shores echoed no sound but the dash of the waves and the lowing of the herds that slaked their thirst in the crystal waters."

" Life and beauty were everywhere, and man, the great destroyer, had not yet come; but not all was peace and harmony in this Arcadia. The forces of nature are always at war, and redundant life compels abundant death. The innumerable species of animals and plants had each its hereditary enemy, and the struggle of life was so sharp and bitter that in the lapse of ages many genera and species were blotted out forever. * * Yielding to the slow-acting but irresistible forces of nature, each in succession of these various animal forms has disappeared, till all have passed away or been changed to their modern representatives, while the country they inhabited, by the upheaval of its mountains, the deepening of its valleys, the filling and draining of its great lakes, has become what it is."

"These changes, which I have reviewed in an hour, seem like the swiftly-consecutive pictures of the phantasmagoria, or the shifting scenes of the drama, but the æons of time in which they were effected are simply infinite and incomprehensible to us. We have no reason to suppose that *terra firma* was less firm, or that the order of nature, in which no change is recorded within the historic period, was less constant then than now. At the present rate of change—throwing out man's influence—a period infinite to us would be required to revolutionize the climate, flora, and fauna; but there is no evidence that changes were more rapid during the tertiary ages. "

"Every day sees something taken from the rocky barrier of Niagara; and, geologically speaking, at no remote time our great lakes will have shared the fate of those that once existed at the far west. Already they have been reduced to less than half their former area, and the water level has been depressed three hundred feet or more. This process is pretty sure to go on until they are completely emptied. The cities that now stand upon their banks will, ere that time, have grown colossal in size, then gray with age, then have fallen into decadence and their sites been long forgotten; but in the sediments that are now accumulating in these lake basins will lie many a wreck and skeleton, tree trunk and floated leaf. Near the city sites and old river mouths, these sediments will be full of relics that will illustrate and explain the mingled comedy and tragedy of human life. These relics the geologist of the future will doubtless gather and study and moralize over, as we do the records of the tertiary ages."

VI. EARLY STATE HISTORY.

1. Alabama.—Capital, Montgomery; Area, 50,722 square miles; Population, (1870,) 996,992. Alabama was settled by the French at Mobile in 1713. It was a part of Georgia until 1802, and then included in Mississippi until March 3, 1817. It was admitted into the Union as a state, by act of Congress, December 19, 1819.

2. Alaska.—Capital, Sitka; Area, 577,390 square miles; Population, (1870,) 70,461. Alaska comprises that portion of North America which is situated north of the parallel of 54° 40′ north latitude, and west of the meridian of 141° west longitude. It embraces numerous islands lying along the coast and extending west from the principal peninsula. It was ceded to the United States by the

Emperor of Russia, for the sum of $7,200,000, by a treaty concluded at Washington, March 30, 1867, and ratified by the Senate, May 28 of the same year.

3. **Arizona.**—Capital, Phœnix; Area, 113,916 square miles; Population, (1870,) 9,658. Arizona was organized as a territory February 24, 1863, from the western part of New Mexico.

4. **Arkansas.**—Capital, Little Rock; Area, 52,198 square miles; Population, (1870,) 484,471. Arkansas was settled by the French at Arkansas Post in 1685, was formed into a territory from a part of Missouri, March 2, 1819, and admitted into the Union as a State, June 15, 1836.

5. **California.**—Capital, Sacramento; Area, 188,981 square miles; Population, (1870,) 560,247. California was settled by the Spaniards at San Diego in 1769, and at San Francisco in 1776. It was ceded to the United States by Mexico in 1848, and admitted to the Union as a State in 1850.

6. **Colorado.**—Capital, Denver; Area, 104,500 square miles; Population, (1870,) 39,864. Colorado was organized as a territory February 28, 1861, and admitted as a State August 1, 1876.

7. **Connecticut.**—Capital, Hartford; Area, 4,750 square miles; Population, (1870,) 537,454. This state includes the original colonies of Connecticut and New Haven. The Connecticut Colony was settled in 1633, at Windsor, and in 1635, at Hartford and Wethersfield, by persons from Massachusetts; and the New Haven Colony in 1638, by a company from England. Separate governments were maintained until the colonies were united by the charter of Charles II, in 1662.

8. Dakota.—Capital, Yankton; Area, 150,932 square miles; Population, (1870,) 14,181. Dakota was organized as a territory, by an act of Congress passed March 2, 1861. The western portion was set off in 1868, to constitute the territory of Wyoming.

9. Delaware.—Capital, Dover; Area, 2,120 square miles; Population, (1870,) 125,015. Delaware was settled by the Swedes and Finns at Wilmington, in 1627; it was subjected by the Dutch of New York in 1655, but fell into the hands of the English in 1664. It was included in the grant to William Penn in 1662, remained a part of Pennsylvania until 1703, and was afterwards under the same government until the adoption of a state constitution, September 20, 1776. It was one of the original thirteen states, and ratified the United States Constitution, December 7, 1787.

10. Florida.—Capital, Tallahassee; Area, 59,268 square miles; Population, (1870,) 187,748. Florida was settled in 1565, by the Spaniards, at St. Augustine, was organized as a territory, March 3, 1823, and admitted into the Union as a State, March 3, 1845.

11. Georgia.—Capital, Atlanta; Area, 58,000 square miles; Population, (1870,) 1,184,189. Georgia was settled at Savannah in 1733, by the English, under General Oglethorpe. It received its charter, June 9, 1732, from George II, from whom it was named. It was the last settled of the original thirteen states, formed its constitution in 1777, and ratified the Constitution of the United States, January 2, 1788.

12. Idaho.—Capital, Boisé City; Area, 86,294 square miles; Population, (1870,) 14,999. Idaho was organized as a territory by Congress, March 3, 1863. It was formed from portions of Nebraska, Oregon, Utah, and Washington territories, but its boundaries were changed at the following session of Congress and a portion of the original territory was included in Montana.

13. **Illinois.**—Capital, Springfield; Area, 55,410 square miles; Population, (1870,) 2,539,891. Illinois was settled at Kaskaskia, by the French in 1683, and was claimed by France until the treaty of Paris, in 1763, when it fell into the hands of the English. Soon after, settlers from Virginia located in the territory, which came under the government of the United States by the war of the revolution. It formed a part of the North-western Territory ceded by Virginia to the United States in 1783, was a part of Indiana as organized in 1800, from which it was separated, and made into a distinct territory in 1809. Its state constitution was framed in 1818, and it was admitted into the Union, December 23, of that year.

14. **Indiana.**—Capital, Indianapolis; Area, 33,809 square miles; Population, (1870,) 1,680,637. Indiana was settled at Vincennes, by French emigrants from Canada, about 1730. It was organized into a territory, May 7, 1800, from which Michigan was set off in 1805, and Illinois in 1809. Its constitution was adopted June 29, 1816, and the State was admitted into the Union December 11, of the same year.

15. **Indian Territory.**—Capital, Tahlequah; Area, 68,991 square miles; Population, (1870,) 68,152. The Indian Territory has been set apart by the Government of the United States as a permanent home for the aboriginal tribes removed thither from east of the Mississippi River, as well as those native to the territory. The United States exercise no authority over them excepting in certain crimes

perpetrated by them against the whites. They are allowed to live under their own laws, follow their own customs, and indulge in their own modes of life. The land has been ceded to the Indians, each tribe owning the portion allotted to it by the United States.

16. Iowa.—Capital, Des Moines; Area, 55,045 square miles; Population, (1875,) 1,350,544. Iowa was settled at Dubuque in 1778, by a colony from Prairie Du Chien, which remained over twenty years. Permanent settlements were commenced about 1830, at Burlington and Dubuque, by emigrants from Michigan and Illinois. It was separated from Wisconsin and organized as a territory by act of Congress in June, 1838, and was admitted into the Union as a State, December 25, 1846.

17. Kansas.—Capital, Topeka; Area, 81,318 square miles; Population, (1875,) 528,349. Kansas formed at different times part of the Missouri, Arkansas, and Indian Territories, from which last it was erected into a separate territory in May, 1854, and admitted into the Union as a State, January 29, 1861. For several years a fierce contest raged in the territory on the subject of slavery, but the strife was finally adjusted by its being admitted as a free State.

18. Kentucky.—Capital, Frankfort; Area, 37,680 square miles; Population, (1870,) 1,321,011. Kentucky was formerly included in the territory of Virginia, was settled in 1774 at Harrodsburg, and was formed into a territory by the Virginia Legislature in 1789. It was admitted into the Union as a State in 1792.

19. Louisiana.—Capital, New Orleans; Area, 41,346 square miles; Population, (1875,) 857,039. Louisiana was first settled by the French at Iberville, in 1699. In

1762, it was ceded by France to Spain, and in 1800, was ceded back by Spain to France.

In 1803, the whole territory included within the "Louisiana Purchase" was ceded by France to the United States. Louisiana was organized as a distinct territory in 1804, and admitted into the Union as a State in 1812.

20. **Maine.**—Capital, Augusta; Area, 35,000 square miles; Population, (1870,) 626,915. Maine was settled at York in 1623 by the English; it was a part of Massachusetts until 1820, when it became an independent State and was admitted into the Union.

21. **Maryland.**—Capital, Annapolis; Area, 11,124 square miles; Population, (1870,) 780,894. Maryland was settled at St. Mary, in 1634, by Roman Catholics, under Cecil and Leonard Calvert. It was one of the original thirteen states, formed a constitution August 14, 1776, and ratified the Constitution of the United States, April 28, 1788.

22. **Massachusetts.**—Capital, Boston; Area, 7,800 square miles; Population, (1875,) 1,651,912. Massachusetts includes the original colonies of Plymouth and Massachusetts Bay; the former was settled at Plymouth, in 1620, and the latter at Salem, in 1628. The colonies remained under separate governments until united by the charter of 1688. Massachusetts was one of the original thirteen states, adopted a constitution in 1780, and ratified the Constitution of the United States in 1788.

23. **Michigan.**—Capital, Lansing; Area, 56,451 square miles; Population, (1874,) 1,334,300. Michigan was settled in 1670, by the French, at Detroit. At the peace of 1763, it came under the dominion of Great Britain. It was a part of the territory ceded to the United States by

Virginia; was set off from Indiana, and erected into a separate territory in 1805, and admitted into the Union as a State, January 26, 1837.

24. **Minnesota.**—Capital, St. Paul; Area, 83,531 square miles; Population, (1870,) 439,706. Minnesota was visited by traders, trappers, and Jesuit Missionaries from Montreal, about 1654. The Upper Mississippi was explored by Louis Hennepin, in 1680. In 1689, a fort was erected by Perrot, Le Sueur, and others, on Lake Pepin, and in 1695 a second fort was established in Minnesota by Le Sueur. In 1812 a settlement was formed in the Red River country, principally by Scotchmen. Fort Snelling was settled by emigrants from the northern and western States about 1845. Minnesota was organized as a territory, March 31, 1849, and admitted into the Union as a State, February 26, 1857.

25. **Mississippi.**—Capital, Jackson; Area, 47,156 square miles; Population, (1870,) 827,922. Mississippi was settled by the Spaniards about the year 1540, and at Natchez by the French in 1716. It was organized as a territory, April 7, 1789, and admitted into the Union as a State, December 10, 1817.

26. **Missouri.**—Capital, Jefferson City; Area, 65,350 square miles; Population, (1870,) 1,721,295. Missouri was settled at St. Genevieve in 1763 by the French. It was organized into a territory, June 4, 1812, and admitted into the union as a State, Dec. 14, 1821.

27. **Montana.**—Capital, Virginia City; Area, 143,776 square miles; Population, (1870,) 20,595. Montana was settled by emigrants from other states, and organized as a territory under an act of Congress approved May 26, 1864. It was formed principally from the northeastern part of Idaho as organized in 1863.

EARLY STATE HISTORY. 59

28. Nebraska.—Capital, Omaha; Area, 75,995 square miles; Population, (1875,) 246,280. Nebraska was settled by emigrants from the Northern and Western States, and was organized as a territory in May, 1854, and admitted into the Union as a State, March 1, 1867.

29. Nevada.—Capital, Carson City; Area, 112,090 square miles; Population, (1875,) 52,540. Nevada was organized as a territory, March 2, 1861, and admitted into the Union as a State, October 31, 1864.

30. New Hampshire.—Capital, Concord; Area, 9,280 square miles; Population, (1870,) 318,300. New Hampshire was settled at Dover and Portsmouth in 1623, by the English. The settlements were annexed to Massachusetts in 1641, and continued until 1679, when New Hampshire received a separate charter. It was again connected with Massachusetts in 1689, but in 1741 it became a separate province. It was one of the original thirteen states, framed a constitution in 1776, and ratified the United States Constitution, June 21, 1788.

31. New Jersey.—Capital, Trenton; Area, 8,320 square miles; Population, (1870,) 906,096. New Jersey was settled at Bergen by the Dutch and Danes in 1624, but it fell into the hands of the English in 1664. In 1674 it was divided into East and West Jersey, and soon after became the exclusive property of the Quakers of Pennsylvania. The two provinces were united in 1702, and the colony was dependent on New York until 1738, when it was erected into a separate royal province. It was one of the original thirteen states, adopted a state constitution July 2, 1776, and ratified the United States Constitution December 18, 1787.

32. New Mexico.—Capital, Santa Fe; Area, 121,201

square miles; Population, (1870,) 91,874. New Mexico was early settled by the Spaniards. It remained a Mexican province until conquered from Mexico and ceded to the United States by the treaty of Guadaloupe Hidalgo, February 2, 1848. It was constituted a territory, with portions of Upper California and Texas, September 9, 1850.

33. **New York.**—Capital, Albany; Area, 47,000 square miles; Population, (1875,) 4,705,208. New York was settled at New York and Albany in 1613 and 1614 by the Dutch, was ceded to the English in 1664, retaken by the Dutch in 1673, and restored to the English at the treaty of Westminister in 1674. It was one of the original thirteen states, framed a constitution in 1777, and ratified the United States Constitution, July 26, 1788.

34. **North Carolina.**—Capital, Raleigh; Area, 50,704 square miles; Population, (1870,) 1,071,361. North Carolina was settled at Albemarle by the English, (emigrants from Virginia,) in 1650, and was chartered, March 20, 1663. It was one of the original thirteen states, adopted a state constitution, December 18, 1776, and ratified the United States Constitution, November 21, 1789.

35. **Ohio.**—Capital, Columbus; Area, 39,964 square miles; Population, (1870,) 2,665,260. Ohio was formed from the North-Western territory, ceded to the United States by Virginia, in 1783. It was settled at Marietta in 1788, by emigrants from New England, and admitted into the Union as a State, April 30, 1802.

36. **Oregon.**—Capital, Salem; Area, 95,274 square miles; Population, (1870,) 90,923. Oregon was first visited by Europeans about 1775. Capt. Robert Gray took possession of it in 1792, naming its principal river after his vessel, the "Columbia," of Boston. The northern bound-

EARLY STATE HISTORY. 61

ary line remained unsettled until the treaty with Great Britain in 1846, when the 49th parallel was adopted. It was organized as a territory, August 4, 1848, was divided March 2, 1852, the northern portion being called Washington, and the southern Oregon. A state constitution was adopted, November 9, 1857, and it was admitted into the Union, February 14, 1859.

37. Pennsylvania.—Capital, Harrisburg; Area, 46,000 square miles; Population, (1870,) 3,521,951. The territory embraced within the present limits of Pennsylvania was granted to William Penn in payment of a debt due his father, Admiral Penn, by the government of Great Britain. In addition to this grant from Charles II, Penn became, by purchase and grant from the Duke of York, the proprietor of the territory now constituting the state of Delaware, and for many years all was united under one government.

Pennsylvania was settled at Philadelphia in 1681, by English Quakers under William Penn. It adopted a state constitution, September 28, 1776, and ratified the Constitution of the United States, December 12, 1787.

38. Rhode Island.—Capitals, Providence, Newport; Area, 1,306 square miles; Population, (1875,) 258,239. This state was settled at Providence in 1636, by the English from Massachusetts under Roger Williams. It was under the jurisdiction of Massachusetts until 1662, when a separate charter was granted, which contiuued to be the basis of the government until the formation of the state constitution in September, 1743. It was one of the original thirteen states, and ratified the United States Constitution, May 29, 1790.

39. South Carolina.—Capital, Columbia; Area, 34,-

000 square miles. Population, (1875,) 925,145. South Carolina was settled by the English at Port Royal in 1670, a grant of the territory having been made in 1662, by Charles II to Lord Clarendon and others.

This is one of the original thirteen states; it established a state constitution March 26, 1776, and ratified the Constitution of the United States, May 23, 1788.

40. Tennessee.—Capital, Nashville; Area, 45,600 square miles; Population, (1870,) 1,258,520. Tennessee was first settled at Fort Donelson, in 1756, by emigrants from Virginia and North Carolina; it originally formed a part of the latter state, but was ceded to the United States in 1784. A constitution was adopted February 6, 1796, and the state admitted into the Union June 1, of the same year.

41. Texas.—Capital, Austin; Area, 274,356 square miles. Population, (1870,) 818,579. Texas was settled at Bexar, now San Antonio, in 1694, by Spaniards; it formed a part of Mexico until 1836, when it declared its independence, and instituted a separate government. It was admitted into the Union as a State, by joint resolutions, approved March 1, and December 29, 1845.

42. Utah.—Capital, Salt Lake City; Area, 84,476 square miles; Population, (1870,) 86,786. Utah was erected into a territory, September 9, 1850. It was occupied mostly by wandering tribes until settled by the Mormons in 1847. After their expulsion from their settlement of Nauvoo, in Illinois, they emigrated to this territory, and having located on the borders of Great Salt Lake, assumed a provisional form of government, and gave to their territory the name of the State of Deseret. In 1850, this form of government was surrendered, and the name of the territory changed to Utah.

EARLY STATE HISTORY. 63

43. Vermont.—Capital, Montpelier; Area, 10,212 square miles; Population, (1870,) 330,551. Vermont was settled at Brattleboro, in 1724, by emigrants from Massachusetts and Connecticut, under grants from New Hampshire. It was claimed by both New Hampshire and New York, and was for a time under the government of the latter, but at a convention held in Westminister, January 16, 1777, it was declared a free and independent state. It was admitted into the Union in 1791.

44. Virginia.—Capital, Richmond; Area, 38,352 square miles; Population, (1870,) 1,225,163. Virginia was settled at Jamestown in 1607 by the English. It was one of the original thirteen states, framed a state constitution July 5, 1776, and ratified the United States Constitution June 25, 1788.

45. Washington.—Capital, Olympia; Area, 69,994 square miles; Population, (1870,) 23,955. Washington Territory was settled by emigrants from the Northern and Western states. It was organized as a territory from the northern part of Oregon, March 2, 1853.

46. West Virginia.—Capital, Wheeling; Area, 23,000 square miles; Population, (1870,) 442,014. West Virginia formed a part of Virginia until 1861, when it separated and framed a constitution for a new state, and was admitted to the Union June 20, 1863.

47. Wisconsin.—Capital, Madison; Area, 53,924 square miles; Population, (1875,) 1,236,729. Wisconsin was settled at Green Bay in 1669, by the French; it was a part of the territory ceded by Virginia to the United States, was set off from Michigan, December 23, 1834, organized as a territory, April 30, 1836, and admitted into the Union as a State, May 29, 1848.

48. **Wyoming.**—Capital, Cheyenne; Area, 97,883 square miles; Population, (1870,) 9,118. On the organization of Montana Territory, and the limitation of Idaho to the districts west of the Rocky Mountains, a tract remained south of Montana, which, for want of public organization, was annexed to Dakota. This region, with small portions of Idaho and Utah was constituted the territory of Wyoming, by an act of Congress, approved July 25, 1868.

VII. CLIMATE.

The United States, extending through more than fifty-seven degrees of longitude and twenty-six of latitude, has a great variety of climate, ranging from cool temperate in the north to semi-tropical in the south,—the conditions for different localities always depending upon the influences of latitude, altitude, topographical features, prevailing winds, warm or cold ocean currents, etc. In order to indicate the results of these diverse influences, and, so far as our limits will permit, present such facts as will lead to a correct estimate of the principal conditions of climate, comparisons will be required between different localities, and to some extent with other countries.

The mean annual temperature of the United States is considerably lower, generally, than that for the same latitudes of Europe, the contrast being greatest in the northern part, and decreasing gradually toward the south; but it does not materially differ from that of Asia. The distribution of heat for the different seasons of the year, however, is of so much greater importance that comparisons between yearly measures have little value. For instance, the mean annual temperature of New York is nearly the same as that of Paris, while for the winter months it corresponds to that of Iceland, and for the summer months it closely approaches that of the region of olive groves and orange groves in southern Europe. The daily extremes of temperature, or alternations between day and night, whether excessive or moderate, also constitute important characteristics of climate.

The climate of the United States is highly favorable to a wide range of vegetation, and to the development and growth of civilized communities. Besides a great variety of forest trees and indigenous shrubs and plants, the orange, lemon, fig, olive, sugar-cane, cotton, rice, tobacco, sweet potatoes, Indian corn, and many other tropical and semi-tropical fruits and vegetable productions of great value, have their favored localities; while wheat and other grains, and all the fruits and vegetables of the temperate latitudes are produced in great abundance and perfection. Population has also increased during the last century with a rapidity that has no parallel in modern times.

In the eastern portion the climate presents very great and important contrasts to that of the western portion, and the leading features of each of these divisions require separate notice.

The comparatively equal distribution of moisture through the year, over the vast area east of the 100th meridian, is a distinguishing feature of that division. This moisture comes principally from the tropics, where the intense heat produces a constant and enormous evaporation, and the winds, sweeping up from the Caribbean Sea and Gulf of Mexico, being an abundant supply, distributing it with great uniformity over this entire area, where it is again precipitated in the form of rain and snow.

The heat that produces this evaporation also causes the atmospheric circulation, which carries to the temperate latitudes a very important portion of their supply of

5

warmth. The heated air of the tropics becomes rarefied and rises, and cooler currents flow in from toward the poles to supply its place, while this lighter air flows back in returning currents, and a constant circulation is thus maintained.

Another important agency by which a portion of the excessive heat of the tropics is carried to the cooler latitudes, is that of ocean currents. The Gulf Stream, for example, is an enormous river of warm tropical waters flowing northward, on the surface of the ocean, diffusing its warm and humid influences over the islands of western Europe, and far inland over the coast, imparting to the climate there an exceptionally high temperature, exempt alike from violent extremes of both heat and cold, and making that the most fertile and habitable portion of the eastern continent. But after leaving the Gulf its influences are not felt on the Atlantic coast to any appreciable extent, owing to the easterly course of the atmospheric currents. Western Europe has therefore a much warmer climate than the United States for corresponding latitudes, except for very limited areas.

A narrow belt bordering the Pacific coast, extending from California northward along the coast of Alaska, has a climate similar to that of western Europe, owing to the modifying influences of the Japan current, which carries the warm waters of the China Sea to the eastern coast of the Pacific, and corresponds to the Gulf Stream of the Atlantic. But the warm breezes coming from the Pacific are soon arrested by mountains or abrupt slopes, and do not extend inland as those from the Gulf Stream do over western Europe, the western slopes there being long and gradual like the eastern slopes of our own continent, offering but slight obstruction to the atmospheric currents,

CLIMATE. 67

while our western slopes are all abrupt, and generally form the base of high mountain ranges.

The topographical features of the eastern portion of the United States are extremely favorable to the prevailing abundance and uniform distribution of its rain-fall. As a whole its surface is remarkably symmetrical and level, the principal elevation occurring in the Appalachian Mountains; but the course of the storms of this section is generally in a direction nearly parallel to these ranges, and their influence in controlling the amount of precipitation on either side is very slight. The entire absence of mountain barriers on the south, and of all obstruction to the winds that sweep up from the Gulf, is a feature of the highest importance. Add to these favorable conditions of surface the close proximity of the warm waters of the Gulf, and the wide expanse of more tropical waters beyond it, and all the needful conditions of supply and distribution are brought together in a remarkable degree; the result of which is, that east of about the 100th meridian we have a vast, well-watered area, greatly exceeding in extent any similar area equally as well watered on the face of the globe.

The amount of moisture precipitated annually in rain and melted snow, varies considerably between different localities, even for that portion lying east of the 100th meridian; but this inequality in amount is largely compensated for in the general absence of excessive quantities falling at one time over the less bountifully supplied sections, and in the more nearly equal, and sometimes greater, number of days on which rain falls in such localities, as compared with those more profusely supplied.

The distribution of heat and moisture are the principal conditions of climate upon which vegetation depends, and their overshadowing importance will justify a brief exhibit of statistical observations, from a sufficient number of points to indicate the general condition for every part of the country.

The following tables show the mean temperature of the places given for each of the seasons, spring, summer, autumn, winter, and for the year; also for January and July in contrast, and the difference between these months,—the mean summer temperatures of all the places in each table being approximately the same.

PLACES HAVING A MEAN SUMMER TEMPERATURE OF ABOUT 60° F.

	Spr.	Sum.	Aut.	Wint.	Year.	Jan.	July.	Dif.
Eastport, Me.,	40.2	60.5	47.5	23.9	43.0	22.4	62.3	39.9
Williamstown, Vt.,	39.0	61.6	41.6	16.4	39.4	15.5	64.0	48.5
Copper Harbor, Mich.,	38.5	60.8	43.0	21.8	41.0	23.4	63.5	40.1
Astoria, Oregon,	51.1	61.6	53.7	42.4	52.2	43.0	59.5	16.5
San Francisco, Cal.,	57.0	60.1	60.1	51.5	57.2	50.1	57.9	7.8

PLACES HAVING A MEAN SUMMER TEMPERATURE OF ABOUT 65° F.

	Spr.	Sum.	Aut.	Wint.	Year.	Jan.	July.	Dif.
Portland, Me.,	42.8	65.2	48.1	24.7	45.2	22.8	68.2	45.4
Buffalo, N. Y.,	42.7	66.9	47.9	27.4	46.2			
Detroit, Mich.,	45.9	67.6	48.7	26.8	47.2	27.0	67.7	40.7
Chicago, Ill.,	41.9	67.3	48.8	25.9	46.7	23.6	70.8	47.2
Milwaukee, Wis.,	42.3	67.3	51.1	26.0	46.4	25.2	69.8	44.6
Fort Ripley, Minn.,	39.3	64.9	42.9	10.0	39.3	7.9	67.3	59.4
Fort Vancouver, W. T.,	51.9	65.6	53.5	39.5	52.7	40.5	68.7	28.2
Benicia, Cal.,	56.5	67.0	60.6	49.0	58.3	47.0	67.3	20.3

PLACES HAVING A MEAN SUMMER TEMPERATURE OF ABOUT 70° F.

	Spr.	Sum.	Aut.	Wint.	Year.	Jan.	July.	Dif.
Boston, Mass.,	46.3	69.1	51.6	28.9	48.9	27.8	71.6	43.8
New York City,	46.7	71.3	55.8	32.3	51.5	31.6	73.2	41.6
Albany, N. Y.,	46.7	70.0	50.0	26.0	48.2	24.3	72.1	47.8
Trenton, N. J.,	49.4	70.7	52.1	32.0	51.1	30.9	72.8	41.9
Philadelphia, Pa.,	50.3	72.4	54.2	34.1	52.7	32.1	74.7	42.6
Pittsburgh, Pa.,	50.0	71.1	51.4	30.6	50.8	29.1	73.0	43.9
Oberlin, Ohio,	46.6	70.2	51.2	29.2	49.3	28.2	75.5	47.3
Ann Arbor, Mich.,	46.8	69.9	51.3	23.3	47.8	23.6	73.0	49.4
Beloit, Wis.,	45.6	70.9	50.1	24.2	47.7	22.7	73.9	51.2
Prairie Du Chien, Wis.,	48.7	72.3	48.3	21.2	47.6	19.4	75.3	55.9
Muscatine, Iowa,	46.4	68.6	48.9	22.8	46.7	20.2	70.5	50.3
Fort Snelling, Minn.,	45.6	70.6	45.9	16.1	44.6	13.7	73.4	59.7
Fort Benton, Montana,	49.9	72.8	44.5	25.4	48.2	16.5	73.6	57.1
Oregon City, Oregon,	54.0	70.2	54.7	40.2	54.8	39.6	72.3	32.7
Sacramento, Cal.,	50.2	72.8	61.3	46.3	59.9	45.3	73.9	28.6
San Diego, Cal.,	60.0	71.2	64.4	52.3	62.0	51.9	72.7	20.8
Santa Fe, N. M.,	49.7	70.4	50.6	31.6	50.6	31.4	72.6	41.2

CLIMATE. 69

PLACES HAVING A MEAN SUMMER TEMPERATURE OF ABOUT 75° F.

	Spr.	Sum.	Aut.	Wint.	Year.	Jan.	July.	Dif.
Annapolis, Md.,	53.8	75.3	57.8	34.8	55.4	32.3	77.2	44.9
Washington, D. C.,	55.8	76.3	56.4	36.1	56.1	34.1	78.2	44.1
Richmond, Va.,	59.3	77.9	60.4	41.4	59.7	38.7	79.2	40.5
Athens, Ga.,	62.7	76.5	61.4	47.6	62.1	45.5	76.8	31.3
Cincinnati, O.,	53.7	74.0	53.9	33.7	53.8	33.1	76.5	43.4
St. Louis, Mo.,	56.4	76.3	55.0	33.8	55.4	32.9	78.5	45.6
Ft. Leavenworth, Kan.,	53.8	74.1	53.7	29.6	52.8	28.0	76.7	48.7
Salt Lake City, Utah,	51.7	75.9	....	32.1	....	27.1	81.5	54.4
Albuquerque, N. M.,	55.9	74.9	57.3	37.1	56.3	35.8	77.3	41.5

PLACES HAVING A MEAN SUMMER TEMPERATURE OF ABOUT 80° F.

	Spr.	Sum.	Aut.	Wint.	Year.	Jan.	July.	Dif.
Charleston, S. C.,	65.9	79.8	66.5	51.4	65.9	48.1	80.1	32.0
Savannah, Ga.,	67.6	80.9	67.6	53.7	67.2	52.2	81.9	29.7
St. Augustine, Fla.,	68.5	80.3	71.5	58.1	69.6	57.0	80.9	23.9
Key West, Fla.,	75.8	82.5	78.2	69.5	76.5	66.7	83.0	16.3
Pensacola, Ft. Barrancas, Fla.,	68.6	81.6	69.8	54.0	68.7	53.6	82.3	28.7
New Orleans, La.,	70.0	82.3	70.7	56.5	69.9	55.3	82.9	27.6
Baton Rouge, La.,	68.9	81.2	68.2	54.2	68.1	53.5	81.8	28.3
Austin, Texas,	68.0	80.7	68.3	49.0	66.7	46.4	80.7	34.3
Ft. Gibson, Ind. Ter.,	61.0	79.4	61.7	41.1	60.8	40.1	80.7	40.6

MEAN TEMPERATURES IN TROPICAL AMERICA.

	Spr.	Sum.	Aut.	Wint.	Year.	Jan.	July.	Dif.
Vera Cruz, Mexico,	78.0	81.5	78.7	71.9	77.5	71.1	81.5	10.4
City of Mexico,	63.4	65.2	60.1	53.0	60.4	52.5	65.2	12.7
Havana, Cuba,	75.7	84.2	75.5	68.4	75.9	65.4	85.2	19.8
Matanzas, Cuba,	78.9	81.4	79.5	73.4	78.3	73.5	81.5	8.0
Bermuda,	63.7	75.2	71.9	58.8	67.4	58.6	75.7	17.1

MEAN TEMPERATURES IN EUROPE AND ASIA.

	Spr.	Sum.	Aut.	Wint.	Year.	Jan.	July.	Dif.
London, England,	47.6	61.0	50.7	39.2	49.7	37.2	62.4	25.2
Liverpool, England,	46.2	57.6	49.1	40.5	48.4	38.7	58.6	19.9
Edinburgh, Scotland,	45.0	57.1	47.9	38.4	47.1	37.4	58.7	21.3
Dublin, Ireland,	47.2	59.6	53.0	38.8	49.7	35.5	60.7	25.2
Paris, France,	50.6	64.5	52.2	37.8	51.3	35.4	65.6	30.2
Berlin, Prussia,	47.4	61.5	49.2	31.4	48.1	27.7	65.8	38.1
St. Petersburg, Russia,	35.9	60.6	40.3	18.1	38.7	15.7	62.7	47.0
Vienna, Austria,	51.6	69.4	51.2	31.9	51.0	29.3	70.7	41.4
Madrid, Spain,	55.7	74.3	57.5	44.4	58.0	44.7	76.3	31.6
Lisbon, Portugal,	59.6	70.9	62.5	52.5	61.4	52.5	72.1	19.6
Rome, Italy,	57.2	74.2	62.7	46.7	60.5	45.0	76.0	31.0
Palermo, Sicily,	59.1	74.4	66.4	52.5	63.1	51.4	75.7	24.3
Constantinople, Turkey,	52.1	73.3	62.3	41.8	57.4	41.7	76.2	34.5
Jerusalem, Syria,	60.5	73.9	66.5	49.6	62.6	47.7	77.3	29.6
Alexandria, Egypt,	66.5	78.3	73.8	58.5	66.8	57.3	78.5	21.2
Pekin, China,	56.6	77.8	54.9	29.0	52.6	26.0	79.3	53.3
Canton, China,	69.8	82.0	72.8	54.9	69.9	52.5	83.0	30.5
Nagasaki, Japan,	60.1	80.2	65.9	44.9	62.8	43.4	80.2	36.8

MEAN ANNUAL AMOUNT OF MOISTURE PRECIPITATED IN RAIN AND MELTED SNOW.

	Inches.		Inches.
Eastport, Me.,	39	Chicago, Ill.,	40
Concord, N. H.,	42	Milwaukee, Wis.,	29
Burlington, Vt.,	34	Green Bay, Wis.,	34
Boston, Mass.,	43	Muscatine, Iowa,	44
New York City,	43	St. Paul, Minn.,	25
Albany, N. Y.,	40	Fort Ripley, Minn.,	29
Buffalo, N. Y.,	36	Corpus Christi, Texas,	41
Ithaca, N. Y.,	30	San Antonio, Texas,	31
Philadelphia, Pa.,	43	Fort McKavett, Texas,	23
Pittsburgh, Pa.,	34	Albuquerque, N. M.,	9
Washington, D. C.,	41	Fort Selden, N. M.,	7
Norfolk, Va.,	45	Fort Craig, N. M.,	11
Charleston, S. C.,	48	Fort Sill, Indian Ter.,	30
Savannah, Ga.,	49	Fort Leavenworth, Kansas,	15
Augusta, Ga.,	41	Fort Dodge, Kansas,	11
Jacksonville, Fla.,	50	Fort Russell, Wyoming,	7
Tampa, Fla.,	55	Fort Randall, Dakota,	18
Southern Florida,	63	Fort Buford, Dakota,	9
Key West, Fla.,	48	Fort Benton, Montana,	7
Mobile, Ala.,	66	Salt Lake City, Utah,	18
Huntsville, Ala.,	54	Fort Lapwai, Idaho,	15
Plaquemine, La.,	66	Fort Colville, Washington,	26
Baton Rouge, La.,	62	Fort Vancouver, Washingt'n,	45
Jackson, Miss.,	53	Fort Stevens, Oregon,	80
Memphis, Tenn.,	42	Camp Warner, Oregon,	8
Louisville, Ky.,	48	Fort Bidwell, Cal.,	10
Cincinnati, Ohio,	47	San Francisco, Cal.,	23
Marietta, Ohio,	41	Sacramento, Cal.,	22
Detroit, Mich.,	30	San Diego, Cal.,	10
St. Louis, Mo.,	42	Fort Yuma, Cal.,	4

It will be seen from the foregoing tables that the summers, nearly everywhere, have high temperatures, closely approaching those of the tropics. They partake largely of a semi-tropical character, while alternating with low winter temperatures, and having other features peculiar to temperate climates. The extreme heat, except in the more elevated portions, closely approaches to or exceeds 100° Fahrenheit, and in some localities it frequently reaches 115° or 120°.

But the effect of the high temperatures, which if continuous would render the summers thoroughly tropical, is greatly modified east of the 100th meridian by the frequent rains that occur, and by other influences that produce intervening periods of lower temperature, so that not more than three or four successive days of extreme heat is usual, especially in the more northern portions. But the nights are generally warm, and the more decidedly tropical characteristics of the southern portion extend over the greater part of this area, though in a more modified form, and for briefer intervals.

The semi-tropical character of its summers is very clearly seen in a wide range of tropical and semi-tropical productions. While the orange, and other tropical fruits are confined to a limited area in the southern portion, owing to the low winter temperatures, the sugar-cane, cotton and rice flourish five to eight degrees further north, and Indian corn, which in Europe is limited to a small area in the southern part, flourishes here over this entire region, except in the more elevated portions, and is cultivated much more extensively than in any other part of the world. A brief period, at least, of hot nights is indispensable to the maturity of this plant, especially in the more northern portions; and this is an important characteristic of the climate east of the dry plains, and one which is found in but limited areas elsewhere.

Over the arid portions west of the 100th meridian, the day temperatures, while fully as high as for the same latitudes on the Atlantic coast, are followed by decidedly cooler nights, the daily range there seldom amounting to less than 20° or 30°, while it sometimes reaches more than 50° in the higher altitudes, where currents of cool air, descending from the snowy regions in the mountains, may cause a day temperature of 80° or 90° to sink to the freezing point during the night. The great daily range of temperature over this part of the continent is owing chiefly to the conditions of altitude, proximity to mountains, and to the great radiation of heat during the night, peculiar to all arid climates. In consequence of the very cool nights, comparatively small areas west of the Rocky Mountains are well adapted to the cultivation of Indian corn, even with the aid of irrigation, though wheat, barley, and oats flourish well where the soil is suitable.

In California, where the seasons are for the most part divided into wet and dry, wheat is produced in great abundance without the aid of irrigation. The wet season commences early in November and continues for a period of about six months, followed by a dry and nearly rainless season for the other half of the year. The wet season is not one of constant rains, but of rains occurring at intervals more or less frequent, similar to the summers of the Atlantic coast. Wheat sown after the early November rains set in,—which are usually followed by two or three weeks of fair weather,—continues to grow all winter, and reaches such a state of maturity during the early spring that it only requires the hot, dry weather of summer to ripen it. The dry summer climate of California is admirably suited to the cultivation of the grape, and in the southern part the almond, fig, orange, and lemon, as well as the more delicate varieties of the grape, are successfully cultivated.

The tables of mean temperature, in connection with that giving the precipitation of moisture, at various points, furnish a condensed exhibit of both of these conditions of climate for nearly every part of the country. These statistics are taken in most instances from observations extending through long periods of years, and will be found to correspond very closely with any extended series of observations for the same localities.

The distribution of moisture over the western plateau, from the Rocky Mountains to the Sierra Nevada, a large area, from which statistics for but a few points are attainable, is very unequal. Not only do the heaviest of the winter snows fall in the mountains, but the summer showers, which are quite frequent in some localities, are confined almost entirely to the mountains, so that cultivation without irrigation is impossible over nearly the whole of this wide extent. In New Mexico and Arizona the summer rains are mostly periodic, partaking somewhat of a tropical character, but are entirely inadequate for purposes of cultivation. In southwestern Texas, while the summer rains are frequently very profuse, causing the streams to overflow their banks, periods of severe drouth are so common as to render success in agriculture nearly impossible. Very heavy rains are characteristic of the Gulf states, but occur with less frequency with the increase of latitude, though extending even beyond our northern boundary. They are so powerful and so frequent in nearly all of the southern states as to render it difficult, in many places, to utilize with safety the water power of the streams for manufacturing purposes.

The remarkably low summer temperature of San Francisco and adjacent portions of the Pacific coast, is owing to a cold, submerged ocean current coming down from the Arctic sea, and rising to the surface near the coast in that locality. The effect of this cold stream, in modifying the summer temperature in this vicinity, though comparatively limited in extent, is as marked as that of the warm Japan current in modifying the winter temperature along the entire Pacific coast of North America.

NAMES OF THE ORIGINAL THIRTEEN STATES.

1 New Hampshire,
2 Massachusetts,
3 Rhode Island,
4 Connecticut,
5 New York,
6 New Jersey,
7 Pennsylvania,

8 Delaware,
9 Maryland,
10 Virginia,
11 North Carolina,
12 South Carolina,
13 Georgia.

AREA OF THE STATES AND TERRITORIES, AS FURNISHED BY THE GENERAL LAND OFFICE AT WASHINGTON.

States and Territories.	Square Miles.	States and Territories.	Square Miles.
Alabama,	50,722	Indian Territory,	68,991
Alaska,	577,390	Iowa,	55,045
Arizona,	113,916	Kansas,	81,318
Arkansas,	52,198	Kentucky,	37,680
California,	188,981	Louisiana,	41,346
Colorado,	104,500	Maine,	35,000
Connecticut,	4,750	Maryland,	11,124
Dakota,	150,932	Massachusetts,	7,800
Delaware,	2,120	Michigan,	56,451
District of Columbia,	60	Minnesota,	83,531
Florida,	59,268	Mississippi,	47,156
Georgia,	58,000	Missouri,	65,350
Idaho,	86,294	Montana,	143,776
Illinois,	55,410	Nebraska,	75,995
Indiana,	33,809	Nevada,	112,090
New Hampshire,	9,280	Texas,	274,356
New Jersey,	8,320	Utah,	84,476
New Mexico,	121,201	Vermont,	10,212
New York,	47,000	Virginia,	38,352
North Carolina,	50,704	Washington,	69,994
Ohio,	39,964	West Virginia,	23,000
Oregon,	95,274	Wisconsin,	53,924
Pennsylvania,	46,000	Wyoming,	97,883
Rhode Island,	1,306		
South Carolina,	34,000	Total,	3,611,849
Tennessee,	45,600		

ALPHABETICAL INDEX.

ALPHABETICAL LIST OF COUNTIES BY STATES AND TERRITORIES.
NUMBERED IN ORDER OF LOCALITY.

ALABAMA.		ALABAMA—Contin'd.		ARKANSAS.	
Counties.	No.	Counties.	No.	Counties.	No.
Autauga,	35	Lawrence,	7	Arkansas,	52
Baker,	34	Lee,	46	Ashley,	71
Baldwin,	59	Limestone,	2	Baxter,	5
Barbour,	57	Lowndes,	43	Benton,	1
Bibb,	32	Macon,	45	Boone,	3
Blount,	13	Madison,	3	Bradley,	66
Bullock,	56	Marengo,	41	Calhoun,	65
Butler,	53	Marion,	11	Carroll,	2
Calhoun,	21	Marshall,	9	Chicot,	72
Chambers,	39	Mobile,	58	Clarke,	56
Cherokee,	15	Monroe,	51	Clayton,	11
Choctaw,	40	Montgomery,	44	Columbia,	69
Clarke,	49	Morgan,	8	Conway,	28
Clay,	27	Perry,	33	Craighead,	20
Cleburne,	22	Pickens,	23	Crawford,	23
Coffee,	62	Pike,	55	Crittenden,	34
Colbert,	5	Randolph,	28	Cross,	32
Conecuh,	52	Russell,	47	Dallas,	57
Coosa,	36	St. Clair,	20	Desha,	60
Covington,	61	Sanford,	16	Dorsey,	58
Crenshaw,	54	Shelby,	25	Drew,	67
Dale,	64	Sumter,	29	Faulkner,	29
Dallas,	42	Talladega,	26	Franklin,	24
De Kalb,	10	Tallapoosa,	38	Fulton,	6
Elmore,	37	Tuscaloosa,	24	Grant,	50
Escambia,	60	Walker,	18	Greene,	12
Etowah,	14	Washington,	48	Hempstead,	62
Fayette,	17	Wilcox,	50	Hot Springs,	49
Franklin,	6	Winston,	12	Howard,	54
Geneva,	63			Independence,	18
Greene,	30	ARIZONA.		Izard,	7
Hale,	31	Maricopa,	4	Jackson,	19
Henry,	65	Mohave,	1	Jefferson,	51
Jackson,	4	Pima,	5	Johnson,	25
Jefferson,	19	Yavapai,	2	Lafayette,	68
Lauderdale,	1	Yuma,	3	Lawrence,	9

ALPHABETICAL INDEX—COUNTIES.

ARKANSAS–Contin'd.		CALIFORNIA–Cont'd.		COLORADO–Contin'd.	
Counties.	No.	Counties.	No.	Counties.	No.
Lee,	44	Lake,	11	Lake,	13
Lincoln,	59	Lassen,	7	Larimer,	2
Little River,	61	Los Angeles,	49	Las Animas,	21
Lonoke,	41	Marin,	20	Park,	10
Madison,	14	Mariposa,	39	Pueblo,	16
Marion,	4	Mendocino,	10	Saguache,	14
Mississippi,	22	Merced,	38	Summit,	1
Monroe,	43	Mono,	42	Weld,	4
Montgomery,	47	Monterey,	40		
Nevada,	63	Napa,	21	**CONNECTICUT.**	
Newton,	15	Nevada,	17	Fairfield,	5
Quachita,	64	Placer,	18	Hartford,	2
Perry,	39	Plumas,	9	Litchfield,	1
Phillips,	45	Sacramento,	24	Middlesex,	7
Pike,	55	San Bernardino,	50	New Haven,	6
Poinsett,	21	San Diego,	51	New London,	8
Polk,	46	San Francisco,	27	Tolland,	3
Pope,	26	San Joaquin,	29	Windham,	4
Prairie,	42	San Luis Obispo,	44		
Pulaski,	40	San Mateo,	32	**DAKOTA.**	
Randolph,	10	Santa Barbara,	47	Armstrong,	75
St. Francis,	33	Santa Clara,	35	Ashmore,	39
Saline,	48	Santa Cruz,	34	Beadle,	34
Sarber,	37	Shasta,	6	Bonhomme,	80
Scott,	36	Sierra,	16	Boreman,	29
Searcy,	16	Siskiyou,	3	Bottineau,	4
Sebastian,	35	Solano,	23	Bramble,	57
Sevier,	53	Sonoma,	19	Brookings,	60
Sharp,	8	Stanislaus,	36	Buffalo,	52
Stone,	17	Sutter,	14	Burbank,	25
Union,	70	Tehama,	8	Burchard,	53
Van Buren,	27	Trinity,	5	Burleigh,	20
Washington,	13	Tulare,	43	Campbell,	30
White,	30	Tuolumne,	37	Cass,	27
Woodruff,	31	Ventura,	48	Cavileer,	6
Yell,	38	Yolo,	22	Charles Mix,	73
		Yuba,	15	Clark,	45
CALIFORNIA.				Clay,	82
Alameda,	33	**COLORADO.**		Cragin,	65
Alpine,	31	Arapahoe,	8	Davison,	66
Amador,	26	Bent,	17	Douglas,	74
Butte,	13	Boulder,	3	Duel,	48
Calaveras,	30	Clear Creek,	6	Edmunds,	33
Colusa,	12	Conejos,	18	Faulk,	41
Contra Costa,	28	Costilla,	19	Foster,	17
Del Norte,	1	Douglas,	9	French,	14
El Dorado,	25	El Paso,	11	Gingras,	15
Fresno,	41	Fremont,	15	Grand Forks,	18
Humboldt,	4	Gilpin,	5	Grant,	47
Inyo,	46	Greenwood,	12	Greeley,	37
Kern,	45	Huerfano,	20	Gregory,	72
Klamath,	2	Jefferson,	7	Hamlin,	46

ALPHABETICAL INDEX—COUNTIES.

DAKOTA—Contin'd.

Counties.	No.
Hand,	42
Hanson,	67
Howard,	8
Hughes,	50
Hutchinson,	76
Hyde,	51
Kidder,	21
Kingsbury,	55
Lake,	59
La Moure,	24
Lincoln,	78
Logan,	22
Lyman,	64
McCook,	68
McHenry,	12
McPherson,	32
Mercer,	11
Meyer,	70
Mills,	35
Miner,	56
Minnehaha,	69
Montraille,	2
Moody,	61
Morton,	19
Pembina,	7
Pratt,	62
Presho,	63
Ramsey,	16
Ransom,	26
Renville,	3
Richland,	28
Rollette,	5
Rush,	38
Sheridan,	13
Spink,	44
Stanley,	49
Stevens,	10
Stone,	36
Stutsman,	23
Sully,	40
Thompson,	43
Todd,	79
Tripp,	71
Turner,	77
Union,	83
Wallette,	1
Walworth,	31
Wetmore,	54
Williams,	9
Wood,	58
Yankton,	81

DELAWARE.

Counties.	No.
Kent,	2
New Castle,	1
Sussex,	3

FLORIDA.

Alachua,	23
Baker,	20
Bradford,	24
Brevard,	36
Calhoun,	7
Clay,	25
Columbia,	19
Dade,	39
Duval,	22
Escambia,	1
Franklin,	9
Gadsden,	10
Hamilton,	16
Hernando,	31
Hillsboro,	34
Holmes,	4
Jackson,	6
Jefferson,	13
La Fayette,	13
Leon,	11
Levy,	28
Liberty,	8
Madison,	14
Manatee,	37
Marion,	29
Monroe,	38
Nassau,	21
Orange,	33
Polk,	35
Putnam,	26
St. John's,	27
Santa Rosa,	2
Sumter,	32
Suwannee,	17
Taylor,	15
Volusia,	30
Wakulla,	12
Walton,	3
Washington,	5

GEORGIA.

Appling,	104
Baker,	124
Baldwin,	70
Banks,	24
Bartow,	19
Berrien,	131

GEORGIA—Continued.

Counties.	No.
Bibb,	78
Brooks,	130
Bryan,	106
Bullock,	96
Burke,	73
Butts,	56
Calhoun,	122
Camden,	136
Campbell,	39
Carroll,	37
Catoosa,	3
Charlton,	135
Chatham,	107
Chattahoochie,	85
Chattooga,	11
Cherokee,	20
Clarke,	46
Clay,	109
Clayton,	40
Clinch,	134
Cobb,	29
Coffee,	115
Colquitt,	129
Columbia,	63
Coweta,	53
Crawford,	77
Dade,	1
Dawson,	14
Decatur,	127
De Kalb,	31
Dodge,	92
Dooly,	101
Dougherty,	123
Douglas,	38
Early,	121
Echols,	133
Effingham,	97
Elbert,	35
Emanuel,	82
Fannin,	7
Fayette,	54
Floyd,	18
Forsyth,	22
Franklin,	25
Fulton,	30
Gilmer,	6
Glascock,	61
Glynn,	119
Gordon,	12
Greene,	48
Gwinnett,	32
Habersham,	17

ALPHABETICAL INDEX—COUNTIES.

GEORGIA—Continued		GEORGIA—Continued.		ILLINOIS—Continued.	
Counties.	No.	Counties.	No.	Counties.	No.
Hall,	23	Sumter,	100	Clay,	78
Hancock,	59	Talbot,	75	Clinton,	76
Haralson,	36	Taliaferro,	49	Coles,	66
Hart,	26	Tatnall,	95	Cook,	14
Harris,	74	Taylor,	87	Crawford,	74
Heard,	52	Telfair,	103	Cumberland,	67
Henry,	41	Terrell,	111	De Kalb,	11
Houston,	90	Thomas,	128	De Witt,	47
Irwin,	114	Towns,	9	Douglas,	56
Jackson,	33	Troup,	65	Du Page,	13
Jasper,	57	Twiggs,	79	Edgar,	57
Jefferson,	72	Union,	8	Edwards,	85
Johnson,	81	Upson,	76	Effingham,	72
Jones,	69	Walker,	2	Fayette,	71
Laurens,	93	Walton,	44	Ford,	41
Lee,	112	Ware,	116	Franklin,	89
Liberty,	105	Warren,	60	Fulton,	37
Lincoln,	51	Washington,	71	Gallatin,	95
Lowndes,	132	Wayne,	116	Greene,	59
Lumpkin,	15	Webster,	99	Grundy,	22
McDuffie,	62	White,	16	Hamilton,	90
McIntosh,	120	Whitfield,	4	Hancock,	34
Macon,	89	Wilcox,	102	Hardin,	99
Madison,	34	Wilkes,	50	Henderson,	25
Marion,	86	Wilkinson,	80	Henry,	17
Meriwether,	66	Worth,	113	Iroquois,	33
Miller,	125			Jackson,	92
Milton,	21	**IDAHO.**		Jasper,	73
Mitchell,	126	Ada,	6	Jefferson,	83
Monroe,	68	Alturas,	8	Jersey,	60
Montgomery,	94	Boise,	7	Jo Daviess,	1
Morgan,	45	Idaho,	5	Johnson,	97
Murray,	5	Kootenai,	1	Kane,	12
Muscogee,	84	Lemhi,	4	Kankakee,	24
Newton,	43	Nez Perce,	3	Kendall,	21
Oglethorpe,	47	Oneida,	10	Knox,	27
Paulding,	28	Owyhee,	9	Lake,	6
Pickens,	13	Shoshone,	2	La Salle,	20
Pierce,	117			Lawrence,	80
Pike,	67	**ILLINOIS.**		Lee,	10
Polk,	27	Adams,	42	Livingston,	52
Pulaski,	91	Alexander,	100	Logan,	46
Putnam,	58	Bond,	70	Macon,	54
Quitman,	108	Boone,	4	Macoupin,	61
Rabun,	10	Brown,	43	Madison,	63
Randolph,	110	Bureau,	18	Marion,	77
Richmond,	64	Calhoun,	58	Marshall,	30
Rockdale,	42	Carroll,	7	Mason,	38
Schley,	88	Cass,	44	Massac,	102
Scriven,	83	Champaign,	48	McDonough,	35
Spalding,	55	Christian,	63	McHenry,	5
Stewart,	98	Clarke,	68	McLean,	40

ALPHABETICAL INDEX—COUNTIES. 79

ILLINOIS—Continued.

Counties.	No.
Menard,	45
Mercer,	16
Monroe,	81
Montgomery,	62
Morgan,	52
Moultrie,	65
Ogle,	9
Peoria,	29
Perry,	88
Piatt,	55
Pike,	50
Pope,	98
Pulaski,	101
Putnam,	19
Randolph,	87
Richland,	79
Rock Island,	15
Saline,	94
Sangamon,	53
Schuyler,	36
Scott,	51
Shelby,	64
Stark,	28
St. Clair,	75
Stephenson,	2
Tazewell,	39
Union,	96
Vermillion,	49
Wabash,	86
Warren,	26
Washington,	82
Wayne,	84
White,	91
Whitesides,	8
Will,	23
Williamson,	93
Winnebago,	3
Woodford,	31

INDIANA.

Counties.	No.
Adams,	27
Allen,	18
Bartholomew,	65
Benton,	19
Blackford,	34
Boone,	33
Brown,	64
Carroll,	21
Cass,	22
Clarke,	84
Clay,	52
Clinton,	30

INDIANA—Continued.

Counties.	No.
Crawford,	90
Daviess,	70
Dearborn,	68
Decatur,	66
De Kalb,	17
Delaware,	41
Dubois,	80
Elkhart,	5
Fayette,	58
Floyd,	92
Fountain,	36
Franklin,	60
Fulton,	13
Gibson,	78
Grant,	33
Greene,	62
Hamilton,	39
Hancock,	48
Harrison,	91
Hendricks,	46
Henry,	49
Howard,	31
Huntington,	25
Jackson,	73
Jasper,	9
Jay,	35
Jefferson,	75
Jennings,	74
Johnson,	55
Knox,	69
Kosciusko,	14
La Grange,	6
Lake,	1
Laporte,	3
Lawrence,	72
Madison,	40
Marion,	47
Marshall,	12
Martin,	71
Miami,	23
Monroe,	63
Montgomery,	37
Morgan,	54
Newton,	8
Noble,	15
Ohio,	76
Orange,	81
Owen,	53
Parke,	44
Perry,	89
Pike,	79
Porter,	2

INDIANA—Continued.

Counties.	No.
Posey,	85
Pulaski,	11
Putnam,	45
Randolph,	42
Ripley,	67
Rush,	57
St. Joseph,	4
Scott,	83
Shelby,	56
Spencer,	88
Starke,	10
Steuben,	7
Sullivan,	61
Switzerland,	77
Tippecanoe,	29
Tipton,	32
Union,	59
Vanderburg,	86
Vermillion,	43
Vigo,	51
Wabash,	24
Warren,	28
Warrick,	87
Washington,	82
Wayne,	50
Wells,	26
White,	20
Whitley,	16

IOWA.

Counties.	No.
Adair,	72
Adams,	82
Allamakee,	11
Appanoose,	97
Audubon,	59
Benton,	52
Black Hawk,	40
Boone,	48
Bremer,	29
Buchanan,	41
Buena Vista,	23
Butler,	28
Calhoun,	35
Carroll,	46
Cass,	71
Cedar,	67
Cerro Gordo,	18
Cherokee,	22
Chickasaw,	20
Clarke,	84
Clay,	14
Clayton,	31

ALPHABETICAL INDEX—COUNTIES.

IOWA—Continued.

Counties.	No.
Clinton,	56
Crawford,	45
Crocker,	5
Dallas,	61
Davis,	98
Decatur,	95
Delaware,	42
Des Moines,	90
Dickinson,	3
Dubuque,	43
Emmett,	4
Fayette,	30
Floyd,	19
Franklin,	27
Fremont,	91
Greene,	47
Grundy,	39
Guthrie,	60
Hamilton,	37
Hancock,	17
Hardin,	38
Harrison,	57
Henry,	89
Howard,	9
Humboldt,	25
Ida,	33
Iowa,	65
Jackson,	55
Jasper,	63
Jefferson,	88
Johnson,	66
Jones,	54
Keokuk,	77
Kossuth,	16
Lee,	100
Linn,	53
Louisa,	79
Lucas,	85
Lyon,	1
Madison,	73
Mahaska,	76
Marion,	75
Marshall,	50
Mills,	80
Mitchell,	8
Monona,	44
Monroe,	86
Montgomery,	81
Muscatine,	68
O'Brien,	13
Osceola,	2
Page,	92

IOWA—Continued.

Counties.	No.
Palo Alto,	15
Plymouth,	21
Pocahontas,	24
Polk,	62
Pottawattamie,	70
Poweshiek,	64
Ringgold,	94
Sac,	34
Scott,	69
Shelby,	58
Sioux,	12
Story,	49
Tama,	51
Taylor,	93
Union,	83
Van Buren,	99
Wapello,	87
Warren,	74
Washington,	78
Wayne,	96
Webster,	36
Winnebago,	6
Winneshiek,	10
Woodbury,	32
Worth,	7
Wright,	26

KANSAS.

Counties.	No.
Allen,	77
Anderson,	61
Arrapahoe,	83
Atchison,	26
Barbour,	92
Barton,	51
Billings,	4
Bourbon,	78
Brown,	12
Buffalo,	67
Butler,	74
Chase,	56
Cherokee,	103
Cheyenne,	1
Clark,	88
Clay,	22
Cloud,	21
Coffey,	59
Comanche,	90
Cowley,	96
Crawford,	102
Davis,	39
Decatur,	3
Dickinson,	38

KANSAS—Continued.

Counties.	No.
Doniphan,	13
Douglas,	43
Ellis,	33
Ellsworth,	52
Foote,	15
Ford,	87
Franklin,	60
Gove,	31
Graham,	17
Grant,	81
Greeley,	45
Greenwood,	75
Hamilton,	64
Harper,	94
Harvey,	72
Hodgeman,	68
Howard,	97
Jackson,	25
Jefferson,	27
Jewell,	7
Johnson,	44
Kansas,	80
Kearney,	65
Kingman,	93
Kiowa,	89
Labette,	101
Lane,	48
Leavenworth,	29
Lincoln,	35
Linn,	63
Lyon,	57
McPherson,	54
Marion,	55
Marshall,	10
Meade,	86
Miami,	62
Mitchell,	20
Montgomery,	99
Morris,	40
Nemaha,	11
Neosho,	100
Ness,	49
Osage,	58
Osborne,	19
Ottawa,	36
Pawnee,	69
Phillips,	5
Pottawatmie,	24
Pratt,	91
Rawlins,	2
Reno,	71
Republic,	8

ALPHABETICAL INDEX—COUNTIES.

KANSAS—Continued.

Counties.	No.
Rice,	53
Riley,	23
Rooks,	18
Rush,	50
Russell,	34
Saline,	37
Scott,	47
Sedgwick,	73
Seward,	84
Sequoyah,	66
Shawnee,	42
Sheridan,	16
Sherman,	14
Smith,	6
Stafford,	70
Stanton,	79
Stevens,	82
Sumner,	95
Thomas,	15
Trego,	32
Wabaunsee,	41
Wallace,	30
Washington,	9
Wichita,	46
Wilson,	98
Woodson,	76
Wyandotte,	29

KENTUCKY.

Counties.	No.
Adair,	109
Allen,	104
Anderson,	28
Ballard,	90
Barren,	105
Bath,	36
Boone,	1
Bourbon,	33
Boyd,	11
Boyle,	80
Bracken,	7
Breathitt,	59
Breckinridge,	45
Bullitt,	48
Butler,	71
Caldwell,	65
Calloway,	96
Campbell,	3
Carroll,	14
Carter,	22
Casey,	79
Christian,	99
Clarke,	34

KENTUCKY—Cont'd.

Counties.	No.
Clay,	87
Clinton,	111
Crittenden,	64
Cumberland,	103
Daviess,	43
Edmonson,	73
Elliott,	23
Estill,	55
Fayette,	32
Fleming,	20
Floyd,	61
Franklin,	29
Fulton,	93
Gallatin,	4
Garrard,	53
Grant,	5
Graves,	94
Grayson,	72
Green,	76
Greenup,	10
Hancock,	44
Hardin,	47
Harlan,	116
Harrison,	17
Hart,	74
Henderson,	42
Henry,	15
Hickman,	92
Hopkins,	66
Jackson,	85
Jefferson,	25
Jessamine,	52
Johnson,	39
Josh Bell,	115
Kenton,	2
Knox,	114
La Rue,	75
Laurel,	83
Lawrence,	24
Lee,	57
Letcher,	89
Lewis,	9
Lincoln,	81
Livingston,	63
Logan,	101
Lyon,	97
McCracken,	91
McLean,	68
Madison,	54
Magoffin,	60
Marion,	78
Marshall,	95

KENTUCKY—Cont'd.

Counties.	No.
Martin,	40
Mason,	8
Meade,	46
Menifee,	37
Mercer,	51
Metcalfe,	107
Monroe,	106
Montgomery,	35
Morgan,	38
Muhlenburgh,	69
Nelson,	49
Nicholas,	19
Ohio,	70
Oldham,	12
Owen,	16
Owsley,	86
Pendleton,	6
Perry,	88
Pike,	62
Powell,	56
Pulaski,	82
Robertson,	18
Rock Castle,	84
Rowan,	21
Russell,	110
Scott,	31
Shelby,	26
Simpson,	103
Spencer,	27
Taylor,	77
Todd,	100
Trigg,	98
Trimble,	13
Union,	41
Warren,	102
Washington,	50
Wayne,	112
Webster,	67
Whitley,	113
Wolfe,	58
Woodford,	30

LOUISIANA.

Counties.	No.
Ascension,	46
Assumption,	48
Avoyelles,	27
Bienville,	11
Bossier,	2
Caddo,	1
Calcasieu,	28
Caldwell,	21
Cameron,	37

ALPHABETICAL INDEX—COUNTIES.

LOUISIANA—Cont'd.

Counties.	No.
Carroll,	8
Catahoula,	22
Claiborne,	4
Concordia,	24
De Soto,	9
East Baton Rouge,	44
East Feliciana,	32
Franklin,	15
Grant,	20
Iberia,	40
Iberville,	42
Jackson,	12
Jefferson,	52
La Fayette,	39
La Fourche,	55
Lincoln,	5
Livingston,	45
Madison,	16
Morehouse,	7
Natchitoches,	18
Orleans,	53
Ouachita,	13
Plaquemines,	56
Point Coupée,	30
Rapides,	26
Red River,	10
Richland,	14
Sabine,	17
St. Bernard,	57
St. Charles,	51
St. Helena,	33
St. James,	49
St. John Baptist,	50
St. Landry,	29
St. Martin's,	41
St. Mary's,	47
St. Tammany,	36
Tangipahoa,	34
Tensas,	23
Terrebonne,	54
Union,	6
Vermillion,	38
Vernon,	25
Washington,	35
Webster,	3
West Baton Rouge,	43
West Feliciana,	31
Winn,	19

MAINE.

Counties.	No.
Androscoggin,	13
Aroostook,	1

MAINE—Continued.

Counties.	No.
Cumberland,	12
Franklin,	6
Hancock,	9
Kennebec,	7
Knox,	16
Lincoln,	15
Oxford,	5
Penobscot,	4
Piscataquis,	3
Sagadahoc,	14
Somerset,	2
Waldo,	8
Washington,	10
York,	11

MARYLAND.

Counties.	No.
Allegany,	2
Anne Arundel,	12
Baltimore,	6
Calvert,	16
Caroline,	18
Carroll,	5
Cecil,	8
Charles,	15
Dorchester,	20
Frederick,	4
Garrett,	1
Harford,	7
Howard,	10
Kent,	13
Montgomery,	9
Prince George's,	11
Queen Anne's,	14
St. Mary's,	19
Somerset,	22
Talbot,	17
Washington,	3
Wicomico,	21
Worcester,	23

MASSACHUSETTS.

Counties.	No.
Barnstable,	12
Berkshire,	1
Bristol,	10
Duke's,	13
Essex,	7
Franklin,	2
Hampden,	4
Hampshire,	3
Middlesex,	6
Nantucket,	14
Norfolk,	9

MASS.—Continued.

Counties.	No.
Plymouth,	11
Suffolk,	8
Worcester,	5

MICHIGAN.

County	No.
Alcona,	25
Allegan,	58
Alpena,	19
Antrim,	16
Barry,	59
Bay,	42
Benzie,	20
Berrien,	71
Branch,	74
Calhoun,	67
Cass,	72
Charlevoix,	12
Cheboygan,	13
Chippewa,	6
Clare,	35
Clinton,	53
Crawford,	23
Delta,	9
Eaton,	60
Emmet,	11
Genesee,	55
Gladwin,	36
Grand Traverse,	21
Gratiot,	46
Hillsdale,	75
Houghton,	2
Huron,	43
Ingham,	61
Ionia,	52
Iosco,	31
Isabella,	40
Jackson,	68
Kalamazoo,	66
Kalcaska,	22
Kent,	51
Keweenaw,	3
Lake,	33
Lapeer,	56
Leelenaw,	15
Lenawee,	76
Livingston,	62
Mackinac,	7
Macomb,	64
Manistee,	26
Manitou,	10
Marquette,	4
Mason,	32

ALPHABETICAL INDEX—COUNTIES. 83

MICHIGAN—Contin'd.		MINNESOTA—Cont'd.		MINNESOTA—Cont'd.	
Counties.	No.	Counties.	No.	Counties.	No.
Mecosta,	39	Fillmore,	78	Waseca,	66
Menominee,	8	Franklin,	27	Washington,	41
Midland,	41	Freeborn,	76	Watonwan,	64
Missaukee,	23	Goodhue,	59	Wilkin,	12
Monroe,	77	Grant,	23	Winona,	70
Montcalm,	45	Hennepin,	38	Wright,	37
Montmorency,	18	Holcombe,	13	Yellow Medicine,	43
Muskegon,	44	Houston,	79		
Newaygo,	38	Isanti,	31	**MISSISSIPPI.**	
Oakland,	63	Itasca,	4	Adams,	56
Oceana,	37	Jackson,	73	Alcorn,	5
Ogemaw,	30	Kanabec,	20	Amite,	64
Ontonagon,	1	Kandiyohi,	45	Attala,	34
Osceola,	34	Lac qui Parle,	42	Benton,	3
Oscoda,	24	Lake,	6	Bolivar,	22
Otsego,	17	Le Sueur,	57	Calhoun,	19
Ottawa,	50	Lincoln,	52	Carroll,	26
Presque Isle,	14	Lyon,	53	Chickasaw,	20
Roscommon,	29	McLeod,	48	Choctaw,	28
Saginaw,	47	Martin,	74	Claiborne,	49
St. Clair,	57	Meeker,	36	Clarke,	54
St. Joseph,	73	Mille Lacs,	19	Coahoma,	16
Sanilac,	49	Monongalia,	35	Colfax,	30
Schoolcraft,	5	Morrison,	17	Copiah,	50
Shiawasse,	54	Mower,	77	Covington,	60
Tuscola,	48	Murray,	62	De Soto,	1
Van Buren,	65	Nicollet,	56	Franklin,	57
Washtenaw,	69	Nobles,	72	Greene,	68
Wayne,	70	Olmsted,	69	Grenada,	25
Wexford,	27	Otter Tail,	16	Hancock,	70
		Pembina,	1	Harrison,	71
MINNESOTA.		Pine,	21	Hinds,	44
Aiken,	10	Pipe Stone,	61	Holmes,	33
Anoka,	39	Polk,	2	Issaquena,	37
Becker,	8	Pope,	26	Itawamba,	15
Beltrami,	3	Ramsey,	40	Jackson,	72
Benton,	29	Redwood,	54	Jasper,	53
Big Stone,	33	Renville,	46	Jefferson,	55
Blue Earth,	65	Rice,	58	Jones,	61
Brown,	55	Rock,	71	Kemper,	42
Carlton,	11	St. Louis,	5	La Fayette,	11
Carver,	49	Scott,	50	Lauderdale,	48
Cass,	9	Sherburne,	30	Lawrence,	59
Chippewa,	44	Sibley,	47	Leake,	40
Chisago,	32	Stearns,	28	Lee,	14
Clay,	7	Steele,	67	Lincoln,	58
Cottonwood,	63	Stevens,	24	Lowndes,	31
Crow Wing,	18	Swift,	34	Leflore,	24
Dakota,	51	Todd,	16	Madison,	39
Dodge,	68	Traverse,	22	Marion,	66
Douglas,	25	Wabasha,	60	Marshall,	2
Fairbault,	75	Wadena,	15	Monroe,	21

ALPHABETICAL INDEX—COUNTIES.

MISSISSIPPI—Cont'd.

Counties.	No.
Montgomery,	27
Neshoba,	41
Newton,	47
Noxubee,	36
Oktibbeha,	29
Panola,	10
Pearl,	69
Perry,	67
Pike,	65
Pontotoc,	12
Prentiss,	6
Rankin,	45
Scott,	46
Simpson,	51
Smith,	52
Sunflower,	23
Tallahatchie,	17
Tate,	9
Tippah,	4
Tishomingo,	7
Tunica,	8
Union,	13
Warren,	43
Washington,	32
Wayne,	62
Wilkinson,	63
Winston,	35
Yallobusha,	18
Yazoo,	38

MISSOURI.

Counties.	No.
Adair,	19
Andrew,	12
Atchison,	1
Audrain,	41
Barry,	98
Barton,	81
Bates,	55
Benton,	57
Bollinger,	94
Boone,	40
Buchanan,	25
Butler,	108
Caldwell,	29
Callaway,	49
Camden,	71
Cape Girardeau,	95
Carroll,	31
Carter,	106
Cass,	43
Cedar,	67
Charlton,	32

MISSOURI—Contin'ed.

Counties.	No.
Christian,	100
Clark,	10
Clay,	28
Clinton,	27
Cole,	48
Cooper,	46
Crawford,	76
Dade,	83
Dallas,	70
Davies,	14
De Kalb,	13
Dent,	75
Douglas,	102
Dunklin,	113
Franklin,	63
Gasconade,	62
Gentry,	4
Greene,	85
Grundy,	15
Harrison,	5
Henry,	56
Hickory,	68
Holt,	11
Howard,	39
Howell,	104
Iron,	91
Jackson,	36
Jasper,	82
Jefferson,	64
Johnson,	44
Knox,	21
Laclede,	72
La Fayette,	37
Lawrence,	84
Lewis,	23
Lincoln,	52
Linn,	18
Livingston,	16
McDonald,	97
Macon,	20
Madison,	92
Maries,	61
Marion,	24
Mercer,	6
Miller,	59
Mississippi,	112
Moniteau,	47
Monroe,	34
Montgomery,	50
Morgan,	53
New Madrid,	111
Newton,	96

MISSOURI—Contin'ed.

Counties.	No.
Nodaway,	2
Oregon,	105
Osage,	60
Ozark,	103
Pemiscot,	114
Perry,	80
Pettis,	45
Phelps,	74
Pike,	42
Platte,	26
Polk,	69
Pulaski,	73
Putnam,	7
Ralls,	35
Randolph,	33
Ray,	30
Reynolds,	90
Ripley,	107
St. Charles,	53
St. Clair,	66
St. Francois,	78
St. Genevieve,	79
St. Louis,	54
Saline,	38
Schuyler,	8
Scotland,	9
Scott,	110
Shannon,	89
Shelby,	22
Stoddard,	109
Stone,	99
Sullivan,	17
Taney,	101
Texas,	88
Vernon,	65
Warren,	51
Washington,	77
Wayne,	93
Webster,	86
Worth,	3
Wright,	87

MONTANA.

	No.
Beaver Head,	8
Big Horn,	11
Chouteau,	5
Dawson,	6
Deer Lodge,	2
Gallatin,	10
Jefferson,	4
Lewis & Clarke,	3
Madison,	9

ALPHABETICAL INDEX—COUNTIES. 85

MONTANA—Contin'd.

Counties.	No.
Meagher,	7
Missoula,	1

NEBRASKA.

Counties.	No.
Adams,	43
Antelope,	6
Boone,	15
Buffalo,	32
Burt,	12
Butler,	24
Cass,	38
Cedar,	3
Chase,	40
Cheyenne,	28
Clay,	44
Colfax,	17
Cuming,	11
Dakota,	5
Dawson,	31
Dixon,	4
Dodge,	18
Douglas,	26
Dundy,	49
Fillmore,	45
Franklin,	54
Frontier,	41
Furnas,	52
Gage,	59
Greeley,	14
Hall,	33
Hamilton,	34
Harlan,	53
Hitchcock,	50
Holt,	1
Howard,	21
Jefferson,	58
Johnson,	47
Kearney,	42
Knox,	2
Lancaster,	37
Lincoln,	30
Madison,	8
Merrick,	22
Monroe,	29
Nemaha,	48
Nuckolls,	56
Otoe,	39
Pawnee,	60
Pierce,	7
Platte,	16
Polk,	23
Richardson,	61

NEBRASKA—Contin'd.

Counties.	No.
Red Willow,	51
Saline,	46
Sarpy,	27
Saunders,	25
Seward,	36
Sherman,	20
Stanton,	10
Thayer,	57
Valley,	13
Washington,	19
Wayne,	9
Webster,	55
York,	35

NEVADA.

Churchill,	8
Douglas,	12
Elko,	3
Esmeralda,	13
Eureka,	10
Humboldt,	2
Lander,	9
Lincoln,	15
Lyon,	7
Nye,	14
Ormsby,	6
Roop,	1
Storey,	5
Washoe,	4
White Pine,	11

NEW HAMPSHIRE.

Belknap,	6
Carroll,	3
Cheshire,	8
Coos,	1
Grafton,	2
Hillsborough,	9
Merrimack,	5
Rockingham,	10
Strafford,	7
Sullivan,	4

NEW JERSEY.

Atlantic,	18
Bergen,	3
Burlington,	14
Camden,	17
Cape May,	21
Cumberland,	20
Essex,	6
Gloucester,	16

NEW JERSEY—Con'd.

Counties.	No.
Hudson,	7
Hunterdon,	8
Mercer,	11
Middlesex,	12
Monmouth,	13
Morris,	5
Ocean,	15
Passaic,	2
Salem,	19
Somerset,	9
Sussex,	1
Union,	10
Warren,	4

NEW MEXICO.

Bernalillo,	8
Colfax,	2
Dona Ana,	13
Grant,	12
Lincoln,	11
Mora,	4
Rio Arriba,	3
Santa Ana,	5
Santa Fe,	6
San Miguel,	7
Socorro,	10
Taos,	1
Valencia,	9

NEW YORK.

Albany,	35
Allegany,	39
Broome,	45
Cattaraugus,	38
Cayuga,	15
Chautauqua,	37
Chemung,	42
Chenango,	30
Clinton,	3
Columbia,	43
Cortland,	29
Delaware,	46
Dutchess,	51
Erie,	22
Essex,	9
Franklin,	2
Fulton,	19
Genesee,	23
Greene,	47
Hamilton,	8
Herkimer,	7
Jefferson,	4

ALPHABETICAL INDEX—COUNTIES.

NEW YORK—Contin'd.

Counties.	No.
Kings,	58
Lewis,	6
Livingston,	25
Madison,	17
Monroe,	13
Montgomery,	32
New York,	56
Niagara,	11
Oneida,	18
Onondaga,	16
Ontario,	26
Orange,	52
Orleans,	12
Oswego,	5
Otsego,	31
Putnam,	53
Queens,	59
Rensselaer,	36
Richmond,	57
Rockland,	34
St. Lawrence,	1
Saratoga,	20
Schenectady,	34
Schoharie,	33
Schuyler,	41
Seneca,	28
Steuben,	40
Suffolk,	60
Sullivan,	49
Tioga,	44
Tompkins,	43
Ulster,	50
Warren,	10
Washington,	21
Wayne,	14
Westchester,	55
Wyoming,	24
Yates,	27

NORTH CAROLINA.

Counties.	No.
Alamance,	24
Alexander,	41
Alleghany,	2
Anson,	85
Ashe,	1
Beaufort,	53
Bertie,	31
Bladen,	88
Brunswick,	93
Buncombe,	62
Burke,	38
Cabarrus,	72

N. CAROLINA—Con'd.

Counties	No.
Caldwell,	39
Camden,	17
Carteret,	91
Caswell,	6
Catawba,	40
Chatham,	47
Cherokee,	55
Chowan,	14
Clay,	57
Cleveland,	68
Columbus,	92
Craven,	82
Cumberland,	77
Currituck,	18
Dare,	34
Davidson,	45
Davie,	43
Duplin,	79
Edgecombe,	29
Forsyth,	22
Franklin,	27
Gaston,	70
Gates,	13
Graham,	56
Granville,	8
Greene,	51
Guilford,	23
Halifax,	10
Harnett,	76
Haywood,	61
Henderson,	64
Hertford,	12
Hyde,	54
Iredell,	42
Jackson,	60
Johnston,	48
Jones,	81
Lenoir,	80
Lincoln,	69
McDowell,	67
Macon,	58
Madison,	35
Martin,	30
Mecklenburg,	71
Mitchell,	37
Montgomery,	74
Moore,	75
Nash,	28
New Hanover,	89
Northampton,	11
Onslow,	90
Orange,	25

N. CAROLINA—Con'd.

Counties.	No.
Pamlico,	83
Pasquotank,	16
Perquimans,	15
Person,	7
Pitt,	52
Polk,	65
Randolph,	46
Richmond,	86
Robeson,	87
Rockingham,	5
Rowan,	44
Rutherford,	66
Sampson,	78
Stanly,	73
Stokes,	4
Surry,	3
Swain,	59
Transylvania,	63
Tyrrell,	33
Union,	84
Wake,	26
Warren,	9
Washington,	32
Watauga,	19
Wayne,	50
Wilkes,	20
Wilson,	49
Yadkin,	21
Yancey,	36

OHIO.

	No.
Adams,	82
Allen,	26
Ashland,	31
Ashtabula,	14
Athens,	77
Auglaize,	36
Belmont,	59
Brown,	81
Butler,	70
Carroll,	47
Champaign,	52
Clark,	53
Clermont,	80
Clinton,	72
Columbiana,	34
Coshocton,	45
Crawford,	29
Cuyahoga,	11
Darke,	50
Defiance,	4
Delaware,	41

ALPHABETICAL INDEX—COUNTIES. 87

OHIO—Continued.

Counties.	No.
Erie,	9
Fairfield,	65
Fayette,	63
Franklin,	55
Fulton,	2
Gallia,	87
Geauga,	13
Greene,	62
Guernsey,	58
Hamilton,	79
Hancock,	17
Hardin,	27
Harrison,	48
Henry,	5
Highland,	73
Hocking,	75
Holmes,	44
Huron,	19
Jackson,	85
Jefferson,	49
Knox,	43
Lake,	12
Lawrence,	86
Licking,	56
Logan,	38
Lorain,	10
Lucas,	3
Madison,	54
Mahoning,	24
Marion,	40
Medina,	20
Meigs,	88
Mercer,	35
Miami,	51
Monroe,	69
Montgomery,	61
Morgan,	67
Morrow,	42
Muskingum,	57
Noble,	68
Ottawa,	7
Paulding,	15
Perry,	66
Pickaway,	64
Pike,	83
Portage,	22
Preble,	60
Putnam,	16
Richland,	80
Ross,	74
Sandusky,	8
Sciota,	84

OHIO—Continued

Counties.	No.
Seneca,	18
Shelby,	37
Stark,	33
Summit,	21
Trumbull,	23
Tuscarawas,	46
Union,	39
Van Wert,	25
Vinton,	76
Warren,	71
Washington,	78
Wayne,	32
Williams,	1
Wood,	6
Wyandot,	28

OREGON.

Counties.	No.
Baker,	22
Benton,	10
Clackamas,	8
Clatsop,	1
Columbia,	2
Coos,	17
Curry,	18
Douglas,	16
Grant,	21
Jackson,	20
Josephine,	19
Lane,	12
Linn,	11
Marion,	9
Multnomah,	7
Polk,	6
Tillamook,	3
Umatilla,	14
Union,	15
Wasco,	13
Washington,	4
Yam Hill,	5

PENNSYLVANIA.

Counties.	No.
Adams,	59
Allegheny,	34
Armstrong,	22
Beaver,	33
Bedford,	55
Berks,	47
Blair,	38
Bradford,	7
Bucks,	66
Butler,	20
Cambria,	37

PENN'IA—Continued.

Counties.	No.
Cameron,	14
Carbon,	48
Centre,	25
Chester,	62
Clarion,	21
Clearfield,	24
Clinton,	15
Columbia,	29
Crawford,	2
Cumberland,	58
Dauphin,	44
Delaware,	63
Elk,	13
Erie,	1
Fayette,	53
Forest,	12
Franklin,	57
Fulton,	56
Greene,	52
Huntington,	39
Indiana,	36
Jefferson,	23
Juniata,	42
Lancaster,	61
Lawrence,	19
Lebanon,	45
Lehigh,	49
Luzerne,	30
Lycoming,	16
McKean,	4
Mercer,	10
Mifflin,	40
Monroe,	31
Montgomery,	64
Montour,	28
Northampton,	50
Northumberland,	27
Perry,	43
Philadelphia,	65
Pike,	32
Potter,	5
Schuylkill,	46
Snyder,	41
Somerset,	54
Sullivan,	17
Susquehanna,	8
Tioga,	6
Union,	26
Venango,	11
Warren,	3
Washington,	51
Wayne,	9

ALPHABETICAL INDEX—COUNTIES.

PENN'IA—Continued.

Counties.	No.
Westmoreland,	35
Wyoming,	18
York,	60

RHODE ISLAND.

Bristol,	2
Kent,	3
Newport,	5
Providence,	1
Washington,	4

SOUTH CAROLINA.

Abbeville,	18
Aiken,	27
Anderson,	11
Barnwell,	28
Beaufort,	32
Charleston,	30
Chester,	7
Chesterfield,	9
Clarendon,	23
Colleton,	31
Darlington,	16
Edgefield,	19
Fairfield,	14
Georgetown,	25
Greenville,	3
Horry,	26
Kershaw,	15
Lancaster,	8
Laurens,	12
Lexington,	20
Marion,	17
Marlboro,	10
Newberry,	13
Oconee,	1
Orangeburg,	29
Pickens,	2
Richland,	21
Spartanburg,	4
Sumter,	22
Union,	5
Williamsburg,	24
York,	6

TENNESSEE.

Anderson,	41
Bedford,	63
Bell,	79
Benton,	29
Bledsoe,	69
Blount,	74

TENNESSEE—Cont'ed.

Counties.	No.
Bradley,	92
Campbell,	17
Cannon,	64
Carroll,	28
Carter,	49
Cheatham,	32
Claiborne,	19
Clay,	12
Cocke,	46
Coffee,	65
Crockett,	52
Cumberland,	39
Davidson,	33
Decatur,	55
De Kalb,	36
Dickson,	31
Dyer,	26
Fayette,	78
Fentress,	15
Franklin,	87
Gibson,	27
Giles,	85
Grainger,	20
Greene,	47
Grundy,	67
Hamblen,	22
Hamilton,	90
Hancock,	21
Hardeman,	80
Hardin,	82
Hawkins,	23
Haywood,	51
Henderson,	54
Henry,	4
Hickman,	57
Houston,	6
Humphreys,	30
Jackson,	13
James,	91
Jefferson,	45
Johnson,	25
Knox,	44
Lake,	1
Lauderdale,	50
Lawrence,	84
Lewis,	58
Lincoln,	86
Loudon,	43
McMinn,	72
McNairy,	81
Macon,	11
Madison,	53

TENNESSEE—Cont'ed.

Counties.	No.
Marion,	88
Marshall,	61
Maury,	59
Meigs,	71
Monroe,	73
Montgomery,	7
Morgan,	40
Obion,	2
Overton,	14
Perry,	56
Polk,	93
Putnam,	37
Rhea,	70
Roane,	42
Robertson,	8
Rutherford,	62
Scott,	16
Sequatchie,	89
Sevier,	75
Shelby,	77
Smith,	35
Stewart,	5
Sullivan,	24
Sumner,	9
Tipton,	76
Trousdale,	10
Union,	18
Van Buren,	68
Warren,	66
Washington,	48
Wayne,	83
Weakley,	3
White,	38
Williamson,	60
Wilson,	34

TEXAS.

Anderson,	71
Angelina,	87
Aransas,	158
Archer,	8
Atascosa,	144
Austin,	123
Bandera,	118
Bastrop,	109
Baylor,	7
Bee,	155
Bell,	80
Bexar,	132
Bexar Territory,	60
Blanco,	106
Bosque,	66

ALPHABETICAL INDEX—COUNTIES.

TEXAS—Continued.

Counties.	No.	Counties.	No.	Counties.	No.
Bowie,	16	Hardin,	114	Orange,	115
Brazoria,	139	Harris,	125	Palo Pinto,	32
Brazos,	96	Harrison,	44	Panola,	56
Brown,	63	Haskell,	17	Parker,	33
Burleson,	110	Hays,	107	Pecos,	59
Burnet,	93	Henderson,	53	Polk,	100
Caldwell,	121	Hidalgo,	167	Presidio,	58
Calhoun,	159	Hill,	67	Rains,	39
Callahan,	46	Hood,	49	Red River,	15
Cameron,	168	Hopkins,	26	Refugio,	157
Cass,	28	Houston,	85	Robertson,	82
Chambers,	126	Hunt,	24	Rockwall,	36
Cherokee,	72	Jack,	20	Runnells,	61
Clay,	9	Jackson,	149	Rusk,	55
Coleman,	62	Jasper,	102	Sabine,	89
Collin,	23	Jefferson,	127	San Augustine,	88
Colorado,	136	Johnson,	50	San Jacinto,	99
Comal,	120	Jones,	29	San Patricio,	164
Comanche,	64	Karnes,	146	San Saba,	77
Concho,	75	Kaufman,	37	Shackelford,	30
Cooke,	11	Kendall,	119	Shelby,	74
Coryell,	79	Kerr,	117	Smith,	54
Dallas,	35	Kimble,	104	Starr,	166
Dawson,	129	Kinney,	128	Stephens,	31
Delta,	25	Knox,	6	Tarrant,	34
Dimmit,	151	Lamar,	14	Taylor,	45
Denton,	22	Lampasas,	78	Throckmorton,	18
De Witt,	147	La Salle,	152	Titus,	27
Duval,	162	Lavaca,	135	Travis,	108
Eastland,	47	Leon,	83	Trinity,	86
Edwards,	116	Liberty,	113	Tyler,	101
Ellis,	51	Limestone,	69	Upshur,	41
El Paso,	57	Live Oak,	154	Uvalde,	130
Encinal,	161	Llano,	92	Van Zandt,	38
Erath,	48	McCulloch,	76	Victoria,	148
Falls,	81	McLennan,	68	Walker,	98
Fannin,	13	McMullen,	153	Waller,	124
Fayette,	122	Madison,	84	Washington,	111
Fort Bend,	138	Marion,	43	Webb,	160
Freestone,	70	Mason,	91	Wegefarth,	2
Frio,	143	Matagorda,	150	Wharton,	137
Galveston,	140	Maverick,	141	Wichita,	5
Gillespie,	105	Medina,	131	Wilbarger,	4
Goliad,	156	Menard,	90	Williamson,	94
Gonzales,	134	Milam,	95	Wilson,	145
Grayson,	12	Montague,	10	Wise,	21
Gregg,	42	Montgomery,	112	Wood,	40
Grimes,	97	Nacogdoches,	73	Young,	19
Guadalupe,	133	Navarro,	52	Young Territory,	1
Hamilton,	65	Newton,	103	Zapata,	165
Hardeman,	3	Nueces,	163	Zavalla,	142

ALPHABETICAL INDEX—COUNTIES.

UTAH.

Counties.	No.
Beaver,	16
Box Elder,	1
Cache,	2
Davis,	6
Iron,	18
Juab,	12
Kane,	20
Millard,	14
Morgan,	5
Piute,	17
Rich,	3
Salt Lake,	8
San Pete,	13
Sevier,	15
Summit,	9
Tooele,	7
Utah,	10
Wasatch,	11
Washington,	19
Weber,	4

VERMONT.

Counties.	No.
Addison,	8
Bennington,	13
Caledonia,	7
Chittenden,	5
Essex,	4
Franklin,	2
Grand Isle,	1
Lamoille,	6
Orange,	10
Orleans,	3
Rutland,	11
Washington,	9
Windham,	14
Windsor,	12

VIRGINIA.

Counties.	No.
Accomack,	39
Albemarle,	26
Alexandria,	9
Alleghany,	22
Amelia,	66
Amherst,	44
Appomattox,	45
Augusta,	17
Bath,	23
Bedford,	63
Bland,	59
Botetourt,	43
Brunswick,	92
Buchanan,	57

VIRGINIA—Contin'ed.

Counties.	No.
Buckingham,	46
Campbell,	64
Caroline,	30
Carroll,	82
Charles City,	52
Charlotte,	89
Chesterfield,	50
Clarke,	2
Craig,	42
Culpepper,	14
Cumberland,	47
Dinwiddie,	68
Elizabeth City,	74
Essex,	33
Fairfax,	8
Fauquier,	6
Floyd,	83
Fluvanna,	27
Franklin,	85
Frederick,	1
Giles,	41
Gloucester,	54
Goochland,	49
Grayson,	80
Greene,	18
Greenville,	93
Halifax,	88
Hanover,	29
Henrico,	51
Henry,	86
Highland,	16
Isle of Wight,	96
James City,	71
King & Queen,	32
King George,	21
King William,	31
Lancaster,	37
Lee,	75
Loudoun,	3
Louisa,	28
Lunenburg,	90
Madison,	13
Matthews,	55
Mecklenburg,	91
Middlesex,	36
Montgomery,	61
Nansemond,	97
Nelson,	25
New Kent,	53
Norfolk,	98
Northampton,	40
Northumberland,	38

VIRGINIA—Contin'ed.

Counties.	No.
Nottoway,	67
Orange,	19
Page,	11
Patrick,	84
Pittsylvania,	87
Powhatan,	48
Prince Edward,	65
Prince George,	69
Princess Anne,	99
Prince William,	7
Pulaski,	60
Rappahannock,	12
Richmond,	34
Roanoke,	62
Rockbridge,	24
Rockingham,	10
Russell,	77
Scott,	76
Shenandoah,	4
Smythe,	79
Southampton,	95
Spottsylvania,	20
Stafford,	15
Surry,	70
Sussex,	94
Tazewell,	58
Warren,	5
Warwick,	73
Washington,	78
Westmoreland,	35
Wise,	56
Wythe,	81
York,	72

WASHINGTON.

Counties.	No.
Chehalis,	8
Clallam,	4
Clarke,	19
Cowlitz,	18
Island,	6
Jefferson,	5
King,	12
Kitsap,	11
Klickitat,	21
Lewis,	16
Mason,	10
Pacific,	9
Pierce,	14
Skamania,	20
Stevens,	2
Snohomish,	7
Thurston,	13

ALPHABETICAL INDEX—COUNTIES. 91

WASHING'N—Cont'ed.
Counties.	No.
Wahkiakum,	17
Walla Walla,	22
Whatcom,	1
Whitman,	3
Yakima,	15

WEST VIRGINIA.
Barbour,	14
Berkeley,	20
Boone,	47
Braxton,	35
Brooke,	2
Cabell,	39
Calhoun,	25
Clay,	43
Doddridge,	11
Fayette,	48
Gilmer,	26
Grant,	16
Greenbrier,	45
Hampshire,	18
Hancock,	1
Hardy,	31
Harrison,	12
Jackson,	33
Jefferson,	21
Kanawha,	42
Lewis,	27
Lincoln,	41
Logan,	46
McDowell,	54
Marion,	6
Marshall,	4
Mason,	32
Mercer,	53
Mineral,	17
Monongalia,	7
Monroe,	51
Morgan,	19
Nicholas,	44
Ohio,	3
Pendleton,	30
Pleasants,	9

W. VIRGINIA—Cont'd.
Counties.	No.
Pocahontas,	37
Preston,	8
Putnam,	40
Raleigh,	49
Randolph,	29
Ritchie,	23
Roane,	34
Summers,	50
Taylor,	13
Tucker,	15
Tyler,	10
Upshur,	28
Wayne,	38
Webster,	36
Wetzel,	5
Wirt,	24
Wood,	22
Wyoming,	52

WISCONSIN.
Adams,	30
Ashland,	3
Barron,	6
Bayfield,	2
Brown,	25
Buffalo,	18
Burnett,	4
Calumet,	36
Chippewa,	7
Clark,	17
Columbia,	43
Crawford,	40
Dane,	49
Dodge,	44
Door,	11
Douglas,	1
Dunn,	14
Eau Claire,	16
Fond du Lac,	35
Grant,	47
Green,	54
Green Lake,	33
Iowa,	48

WISCONSIN—Cont'ed.
Counties.	No.
Jackson,	20
Jefferson,	50
Juneau,	29
Kenosha,	58
Kewaunee,	26
La Crosse,	27
La Fayette,	53
Manitowoc,	37
Marathon,	8
Marquette,	32
Milwaukee,	52
Monroe,	28
Oconto,	9
Outagamie,	24
Ozaukee,	46
Pepin,	15
Pierce,	13
Polk,	5
Portage,	22
Racine,	57
Richland,	41
Rock,	55
St. Croix,	12
Sauk,	42
Shawano,	10
Sheboygan,	38
Trempealeau,	19
Vernon,	39
Walworth,	56
Washington,	45
Waukesha,	51
Waupaca,	23
Waushara,	31
Winnebago,	34
Wood,	21

WYOMING.
Albany,	4
Carbon,	3
Laramie,	5
Sweetwater,	2
Uinta,	1

ALPHABETICAL INDEX—MOUNTAINS.

MOUNTAINS.

	Co.		Co.
Adirondack, N. Y.,	9	Cerbat, Arizona,	1
Ajo, Arizona,	5	Chestnut Ridge, Penn.,	53
Alleghany, Penn.,	25	Chiricahui, Arizona,	5
Alleghany, W. Virginia,	30	Chocolate, California,	51
Amargosa, California,	46	Clan Alpine, Nevada,	8
Antelope, Nevada,	2	Clinch, Virginia,	77
Apache, Arizona,	2	Cœur d' Allene, Idaho,	2
Apache, Texas,	59	Copper Ridge, Virginia,	76
Aquarius, Arizona,	1	Cortez, Nevada,	10
		Cosco, California,	46
Bald Eagle, Penn.,	25	Cove, Penn.,	56
Bald, Montana,	8	Creek, Idaho,	9
Bald. N. Carolina,	67	Cross, Arizona,	2
Battle, Nevada,	2	Cumberland, Ky.,	115
Bear Butte, Dakota, southwest part unorganized.		Dan's, Maryland,	1
Bear Paw, Montana,	5	Dead, Nevada,	15
Bear River, Idaho,	10	Delaware Ridge, Indian Ter., Chickasaw Nation.	
Beauchamp Peak, Arizona,	2		
Belt, Montana,	7	Desatoya, Nevada,	8
Big Flat Top, W. Virginia,	54	Diamond Peak, Oregon,	13
Big Hole, Montana,	1	Diamond Range, Nevada,	10
Big Horn, Wyoming,	3	Dome, Arizona,	3
Big Sewell, W. Virginia,	48	Double, Texas,	1
Bill Williams, Arizona,	2	Dug Down, Georgia,	27
Bitter Root, Idaho,	2		
Black Dome, N. Carolina,	36	Eagle, Texas,	57
Black Hills, Washington,	8	Eagle Tail, Arizona,	3
Black Hills, Wyoming,	3	Egan Range, Nevada,	11
Black Hills, Wyoming,	5	East River, Virginia,	58
Black Log, Penn.,	39	Elkhead Range, Colorado,	1
Black, Arizona,	1	Elk, Colorado,	10
Black Rock Range, Nevada,	2	Ely, Nevada,	15
Blue, N. J.,	1	Eugene, Nevada,	2
Blue, Oregon,	21	Excelsior, Nevada,	13
Blue, Penn.,	47		
Blue Peaks, Arizona,	2	Fisher's Peak, Colorado,	21
Blue Ridge, Georgia,	15	Fork, W. Virginia,	30
Buffalo Ridge, Virginia,	44	Fortification, Arizona,	4
Bull Run, Virginia,	7	Fremont's Peak, Wyoming,	2
Burro, N. Mexico,	12		
Bushy, N. Carolina,	39	Great Monadnock, N. H.,	8
		Ganley, W. Virginia,	48
Cabeza Prieta, Arizona,	3	Gavillan, California,	40
Cabinet, Montana,	1	Goose Creek, Idaho,	9
Cæsar's Head, N. Carolina,	63	Goshute, Utah,	7
Calabasa, Arizona,	2	Grand Father, N. C.,	19
Camel's Hump, Vt.,	9	Granite, Arizona,	3
Carson Sink, Nevada,	8	Granite, Nevada,	1
Cascade, Wash.,	15	Granite, Utah,	7
Catskill, N. Y.,	47	Gray's Peak, Colorado,	7
Cedar, Utah,	7	Great North, W. Virginia,	31

ALPHABETICAL INDEX—MOUNTAINS. 93

	Co.		Co.
Great Savage, W. Virginia,	15	Mt. Dana, California,	37
Great Unaka, Tenn.,	74	Mt. Diablo, California,	28
Greenbrier, W. Virginia,	37	Mt. Fanin, Texas,	1
Green, Vermont,	8	Mt. Gardner, California,	46
Guadalupe, N. Mexico,	13	Mt. Harvard, Colorado,	10
Guyot's Range, Utah,	7	Mt. Hayden, Idaho,	10
		Mt. Hoffmann, California,	37
Heart, Wyoming,	2	Mt. Holyoke, Mass.,	3
Hiko Range, Nevada,	15	Mt. Hood, Oregon,	13
Hot Creek, Nevada,	14	Mt. Hope, Arizona,	2
Hueco, N. Mexico,	13	Mt. Jackson, Virginia,	4
Humboldt, Nevada,	2	Mt. Jefferson, Oregon,	13
Humboldt Range, Nevada,	3	Mt. Katahdin, Maine,	3
		Mt. Kearsarge, N. H.,	5
Iron, Virginia,	78	Mt. Kendrick, Arizona,	2
Inyo, California,	46	Mt. King, California,	46
		Mt. Lyell, California,	42
Judith, Montana,	7	Mt. Lynn, California,	10
		Mt. Madison, Montana,	10
Killington Peak, Vt.,	12	Mt. Mansfield, Vermont,	6
Kingston, California,	50	Mt. Marcy, N. Y.,	9
		Mt. Nebo, Utah,	12
Lapway, Idaho,	2	Mt. Newberry, Arizona,	1
Laramie Peak, Wyoming,	4	Mt. Olympus, Washington,	4
Lassens Peak, Cal.,	9	Mt. Pinos, California,	49
Laurel Hill, Penn.,	53	Mt. Pitt, Oregon,	20
Litite, Utah,	13	Mt. Rainier, Washington,	14
Little Missouri Buttes, Wyom'g,	5	Mt. Ripley, California,	12
Little Rocky, Montana,	6	Mt. St. Helens, California,	11
Long's Peak, Colorado,	2	Mt. St. John, California,	12
Lookout, Georgia,	1	Mt. St. Helena, Washington,	20
Los Pinos, Colorado,	14	Mt. Seward, New York,	2
Luke Ridge, Nevada,	2	Mt. Shasta, California,	3
		Mt. Sheridan, Wyoming,	1
Mars Hill, Maine,	1	Mt. Silliman, California,	43
Mayacamas, California,	10	Mt. Sitgreaves, Arizona,	2
Medicine Bow, Wyoming,	3	Mt. Skomekan, Washington,	1
Miembres, N. Mexico,	12	Mt. Spruce, Nevada,	3
Mill, Virginia,	23	Mt. Stuart, Washington,	15
Mine Ridge, Penn.,	61	Mt. Sunapee, N. Hampshire,	5
Mogee's Peak, California,	6	Mt. Taylor, New Mexico,	9
Mogollon, Arizona,	2	Mt. Tyndall, California,	46
Mojave Ridge, California,	50	Mt. Union, Pennsylvania,	39
Monitor, Nevada,	14	Mt. View, California,	32
Monument, California,	50	Mt. Wachusett, Mass.,	5
Mormon Range, Nevada,	15	Mt. Washington, N. H.,	1
Mt. Adams, Washington,	21	Mt. Whitney, California,	43
Mt. Aiks, Washington,	15	Mt. Yale, Colorado,	10
Mt. Arlington, Oregon,	17	Muddy, Nevada,	15
Mt. Baker, Washington,	1		
Mt. Bullion, California,	39	Nightingale,	2
Mt. Calapooya, Oregon,	12	Nittany, Pennsylvania,	25
Mt. Chuchehehum, Washington,	1	North, Virginia,	24

ALPHABETICAL INDEX—MOUNTAINS.

	Co.
Nuahum Peak, Oregon,	13
Ozark, Arkansas,	3
Pacheco Peak, California,	38
Pahranagat Range, Nevada,	15
Pah Ute, California,	50
Palisades, California,	41
Panoche Peak, California,	41
Panther, Montana,	6
Peaks of Otter, Virginia,	43
Peloncillo, Arizona,	5
Peters, W. Virginia,	51
Pike's Peak, Colorado,	12
Pinaleño, Arizona,	5
Pinal, Arizona,	4
Pine, Kentucky,	116
Pine Nut, Nevada,	12
Piuvon Range, Nevada,	10
Porcupine Tail, Dakota, southwest part unorganized.	
Posey Peak, California,	45
Poteau, Indian Ter., Choctaw Nation.	
Powell's, Tennessee,	21
Providence, California,	50
Pueblo, Oregon,	21
Pumpkin Butte, Wyoming,	4
Pyramid Peak, California,	25
Pyramid Range, N. Mexico,	12
Quien Horn, Wyoming,	2
Quijotoa, Arizona,	5
Quin's River, Nevada,	2
Rabbit, Nevada,	2
Raft, Utah,	1
Raton, Colorado,	21
Resting Spring, California,	50
Reveille, Nevada,	14
Rich, W. Virginia,	29
Roan or Book, Colorado,	1
Roberts Creek, Nevada,	10
Rocky, Idaho,	5
Rogue River, Oregon,	16
Round, California,	6
Saddle, Massachusetts,	1
St. Mary's Peak, Montana,	1
Salmon River, Idaho,	8
San Bernardino Range, Cal.,	51
San Carlos Peak,	41
San Francisco, Arizona,	2
San Juan, Colorado,	14

	Co.
Sans Bois, Indian Ter., Choctaw Nation.	
Santa Anna Peak, Cal.,	40
Santa Inez, California,	47
Santa Lucia Range, Cal.,	40 & 44
Santa Rosa, Nevada,	2
Schooley, New Jersey,	8
Scott's Peak, Oregon,	16
Scotts, California,	2
Shade, Pennsylvania,	40
Shasta, California,	5
Shawney Ridge, Penn.,	30
Shell Creek Range, Nevada,	11
Shoshone, Nevada,	9
Sidling Hill, Penn.,	39
Sierra Blanca, New Mexico,	11
Sierra Blanca, Texas,	57
Sierra Capitana, New Mexico,	11
Sierra Carizo, New Mexico,	11
Sierra de Abo, New Mexico,	10
Sierra de Chusca, N. Mexico,	3
Sierra de Datili, N. Mexico,	10
Sierra de La Plata, Colorado,	10
Sierra del Caballo, N. Mexico,	13
Sierra de Los Pinos, Colorado,	18
Sierra de San Raphael, Cal.,	47
Sierra Diablo, New Mexico,	12
Sierra Florida, N. Mexico,	12
Sierra Madelena, N. Mexico,	10
Sierra Nacimiento, N. Mexico,	5
Sierra Oscaro, New Mexico,	10
Sierra Pajuna, New Mexico,	13
Sierra Sacramento, N. Mexico,	13
Sierra San Fernando, Cal.,	49
Sierra San Mateo, N. Mexico,	10
Sierra San Miguel, Colorado,	10
Sierra Soledad, New Mexico,	13
Silver, Nevada,	12
Silver Peak, Nevada,	13
Sinkawala, Nevada,	14
Siskiyou, California,	1
Snake Range, Nevada,	14
Snow, Oregon,	21
Southwest, Virginia,	18
Spanish Peaks, Colorado,	21
Spring Range, Nevada,	15
Stone, Pennsylvania,	40
Stone, Virginia,	75
Sunday Peak, California,	43
Sweet Water, Wyoming,	2
Table Hills, Wyoming,	2
Taylor's Ridge, Georgia,	11

ALPHABETICAL INDEX—VALLEYS. 95

	Co.		Co.
Telescope, California,	46	Walker's, Virginia,	79
Thomas Ridge, Utah,	7	Warm Spring, Virginia,	23
Touno Range, Nevada,	3	Warner's Range, California,	3
Tollock, Nevada,	13	Wassuck, Nevada,	13
Toquima, Nevada,	14	West Gate, Nevada,	8
Toyabee, Nevada,	14	White, Arizona,	2
Trinity, Nevada,	2	White, California,	42
Tuscarora, Pennsylvania,	57	White, New Hampshire,	1
Tussey's, Pennsylvania,	39	White Pine Range, Nevada,	14
Tussey's, Pennsylvania,	55	Wichita, Indian Ter., southwest part.	
		Wind River, Wyoming,	2
Uintah, Utah,	11	Winter Ridge, Oregon,	20
Umpqua, Oregon,	17	Wolf Creek, Virginia,	59
Uncompahgre, Colorado,	10	Wyoming, Pennsylvania,	30
Vegas Range, Nevada,	15	Yallowballey, California,	5
Virgin Range, Nevada,	15	Young Men's Buttes, Dakota,	9
Wahsatch, Utah,	18	Zuni, New Mexico,	9
Wahweah, Nevada,	9		

VALLEYS.

	Co.		Co.
Antelope, Nevada,	11	Gabbs, Nevada,	13
Artemisia Barrens, Wyoming,	2	Garden, Nevada,	3
		Gila Desert, Arizona,	3
Big Hole Prairie, Montana,	8	Glover, Nevada,	3
Big Meadows, Oregon,	21	Goshute Desert, Nevada,	3
Big Smoke, Nevada,	14	Grande Ronde, Oregon,	15
Black Rock Desert, Nevada,	2	Grass, Nevada,	9
Brown, Alabama,	13	Great Plains, Columbia River,	
Bud, Nevada,	14	Washington,	2, 3
		Hause, Utah,	1
Carnas Prairie, Idaho,	8	Homans Park,	14
Carico, Nevada,	9	Horse Plains,	1
Clover, Nevada,	15	Huerfano Park, Colorado,	20
Colorado Plateau, Arizona,	2	Huevis, Arizona,	1
Crescent, Nevada,	10	Laramie Plain, Wyoming,	3
		Little Smoky, Nevada,	14
Death, California,	50	Long, Nevada,	11
Deer Lodge Prairie, Montana,	2		
Desert, California,	50	Malade, Utah,	1
Desert Plateau, Nevada,	15	Mauvaises Terres, Dakota,	
Diamond, Nevada,	10	southwest part unorganized.	
Duck, Nevada,	14	Meadow, Nevada,	15
		Monitor, Nevada,	14
Edward Creek, Nevada,	8	Mountain Desert, Nevada,	15
Elevated Plateau, Nevada,	3		
Elevated Plains, Utah,	11	National Park, Wyoming,	1
		North Park, Colorado,	1
Fair View, Nevada,	8		
Fish Lake, Nevada,	13	Pahranagat, Nevada,	15
Fish Spring, Nevada,	14	Painted Desert, Arizona,	2

ALPHABETICAL INDEX—LAKES.

	Co.
Panamint, California,	50
Paradise, Nevada,	2
Parter, Utah,	7
Plains of San Augusta, N. M.,	10
Plateau du Coteau, Dakota,	45
Plateau du Coteau du Missouri, Dakota,	33
Prairies, Minnesota,	61
Pueblo, Nevada,	2
Round, California,	7
Sage Plain, Colorado,	18
Sage Plain, Oregon,	21
Salt, Nevada,	8
San Francisco Plain, Arizona,	2
San Luis Park, Colorado,	19

	Co.
Smith's, Nevada,	9
Snake, Nevada,	14
South Park, Colorado,	11
Spring, or Lone Rock, Utah,	7
Steptoe, Nevada,	11
Surprise, California,	3
Vegas, Nevada,	15
Valley de Los Playas, N. M.,	12
Wallapi, Arizona,	1
Walker Lake, Nevada,	13
Warner's, Oregon,	21
White Pine, Nevada,	14
Yosemite, California,	39

LAKES.

Albert, Oregon,	20
Alkali, Nevada,	1
Antelope, Oregon,	21
Baskahegan, Maine,	10
Bear River, Idaho,	10
Beaver, Indiana,	8
Bemidji, Minnesota,	3
Big, Maine,	10
Big Stone, Dakota,	47
Black, New York,	1
Black, Louisiana,	18
Buena Vista, California,	45
Caddo, Louisiana,	1
Canandaigua, N. Y.,	26
Canquomgomoc, Maine,	3
Carson, Nevada,	8
Cass, Minnesota,	9
Cayuga, New York,	28
Cedar, Minnesota,	74
Chamberlain, Maine,	3
Chautauqua, New York,	37
Chazy, New York,	3
Chesuncook, Maine,	3
Christmas, Oregon,	21
Clam, Michigan,	27
Clam, Wisconsin,	4
Clear, California,	11
Cleveland, Maine,	1
Cold Spring, Dakota, Sisseton and Warpeton Indian Res.	
Conesus, New York,	25

Cooper's, Wyoming,	3
Crooked, New York,	40
Cross, Louisiana,	1
Dexter, Florida,	30
Dry, California,	45
Dry, California,	51
Dunn's, Florida,	27
Eagle, California,	7
Elbow, Minnesota,	8
Fall, California,	6
Fish River, Maine,	1
Flat Head, Montana,	1
Fox, Wisconsin,	44
Franklin, Nevada,	3
Goose, California,	3
Grand, Louisiana,	40
Grand, Maine,	10
Great Salt, Utah,	1
Green, Minnesota,	35
Higgins, Michigan,	29
Honey, California,	7
Horicon, Wisconsin,	44
Houghton's,	29
Humboldt, Nevada,	2
Humboldt & Carson's Sink, Nevada,	8
Itasca, Minnesota,	3
Kanicksu, Idaho,	1

ALPHABETICAL INDEX—LAKES. 97

	Co.		Co.
Kern, California,	- 45	Lake Winnebago, Wisconsin,	- 36
Klamath, Oregon,	- 20	Lake Winnipiseogee, N. H.,	3 & 6
		Lake Winthrop, Maine,	- 1
Lake Abert, Dakota,	- 46	Leech, Minnesota,	- 9
Lake Agogebic, Michigan,	- 1	Long, Minnesota,	- 38
Lake Aliapopka, Florida,	- 33	Long, New York,	- 8
Lake Benton, Minnesota,	- 52	Lower Klamath, Oregon,	- 20
Lake Bistineau, Louisiana,	- 11		
Lake Bodeau, Louisiana,	- 2	Madison, Wyoming,	- 1
Lake Borgne, Louisiana,	- 57	Market, Idaho,	- 8
Lake Butler, Florida,	- 24	Mendota, Wisconsin,	- 49
Lake Calcasieu, Louisiana,	- 37	Mermenton, Louisiana,	- 38
Lake Ca'chess, Washington,	- 15	Micha, Minnesota,	- 3
Lake Charles, Louisiana,	- 28	Mille Lacs, Minnesota,	- 10
Lake Chelan, Washington,	- 2	Miniskaja, or Salt Lake, Dakota,	25
Lake Cœur d' Allene, Idaho,	- 1	Mini Wakau, or Devil's Lake,	
Lake Court Oreille, Wis.,	- 7	Dakota,	- 14 & 16
Lake Dora, Florida,	- 32	Mono Lake, California,	- 42
Lake Erie, Ohio, Penn., & N. Y.,	—	Moosehead, Maine,	- 3
Lake Eustis, Florida,	- 32		
Lake Gauss, Minnesota,	- 9	Namekan, Minnesota,	- 5
Lake George, Florida,	- 30		
Lake George, New York,	- 10	Okeechobee, Florida,	- 36
Lake Griffin, Florida,	- 32	Oneida, New York,	- 18
Lake Harney, Oregon,	- 21	Orange, Florida,	- 23
Lake Huron, Michigan,	—	Otter Tail, Minnesota,	- 14
Lake Heron, Minnesota,	- 73	Owasco, New York,	- 15
Lake Istopoga, Florida,	- 37	Owen, California,	- 46
Lake Jesup, Florida,	- 33	Pamedecook, Maine,	- 3
Lake Kampeska, Dakota,	- 45	Pauwaicun, Wisconsin,	- 34
Lake Kissimee, Florida,	- 36	Peoria, Illinois,	- 31
Lake Linne, Dakota,	- 37	Pyramid, Nevada,	- 1
Lake Malhear, Oregon,	- 21		
Lake Maurepas, Louisiana,	- 50	Quinaiutte, Washington,	- 8
Lake McIntosh, Dakota,	- 6		
Lake Menona, Wisconsin,	- 49	Racket, New York,	- 8
Lake Michigan, Michigan,	—	Red, Minnesota,	- 3
Lake Monroe, Florida,	- 30	Rhett, California,	- 3
Lake Okabena, Minnesota,	- 72	Rice, Minnesota,	- 3
Lake Ossipee, New Hampshire,	- 3		
Lake Pend d'Oveille, Idaho,	- 1	Sabine, Texas,	127
Lake Poinsett, Dakota,	- 46	St. Croix, Wisconsin,	- 1
Lake Pontchartrain, Louisiana,	- 53	Salt Lake, Washington,	- 2
Lake Preble, Maine,	- 1	Saranac Lake, New York,	- 2
Lake St. Clair, Michigan,	- 64 & 70	Sebago, Maine,	- 12
Lake Shamano, Minnesota,	- 17	Sebec, Maine,	- 3
Lake Sedowick, Maine,	- 1	Seneca, New York,	- 27
Lake Shetek, Minnesota,	- 62	Sevier, Utah,	- 14
Lake Sunapee, N. H.,	- 5	Seven Beaver, Minnesota,	- 5
Lake Superior, Michigan,	—	Shoshone, Wyoming,	- 1
Lake Thompson, Dakota,	- 58	Silver, Oregon,	- 20
Lake Tohopekaliga, Florida,	- 33	Skaneateles, New York,	- 16
Lake Traverse, Dakota,		Squam, New Hampshire,	- 2
Sisseton & Warpeton Indian Res.		Squawpan, Maine,	- 1

ALPHABETICAL INDEX—RIVERS.

	Co.		Co.
Summer, Oregon,	- 3	Utah, Utah,	- 10
Surprise Valley, California,	- 3		
Swan, Minnesota,	- 56	Vermillion, Minnesota,	- 5
Tchanchicahah, Dakota,	- 34	Walker, Nevada,	- 13
Tchaurarahedan, Dakota,	- 43	White Fish, Minnesota,	- 9
Tulave, California,	- 43	Winibigoshish, Minnesota,	- 4
Tupper's, New York,	- 1	Winnemucca, Nevada,	- 2
		Wright, California,	- 3
Umbagog, Maine,	- 5		
Upper Klamath, Oregon,	- 20	Yellow Stone, Wyoming,	- 1

RIVERS.

	Co.		Co.
Akanaquint Creek, Utah,	- 15	Baptism, Minnesota,	- 6
Alabama, Alabama,	- 59	Barrel Creek, Oregon,	- 13
Allaguash, Maine,	- 1	Bartholomew, Louisiana,	- 7
Allapaha, Florida,	- 16	Baudette, Minnesota,	- 4
Alleghany, Pennsylvania,	- 34	Bayada, New Mexico,	- 4
Alseya, Oregon,	- 10	Bayou Canes, Louisiana,	- 29
Altamaha, Georgia,	119	Bayou d' Arbonne, Louisiana,	- 6
Altoinac, Texas,	- 88	Bayou Deview, Arkansas,	- 43
Amargosa, California,	- 50	Bayou Lafourche, Louisiana,	- 55
Amargosa, Nevada,	- 14	Bayou Lanacoco, Louisiana,	- 25
Ambroisa Creek, Texas,	160	Bayou Nezpigue, Louisiana,	- 29
American Crow Creek, Dakota,	- 64	Bayou Teche, Louisiana,	- 47
American, California,	- 24	Bayou Terribonne, Louisiana,	- 54
Amite, Louisiana,	- 46	Bear Creek, California,	- 38
Androscoggin, Maine,	- 14	Bear, Utah,	- 1
Angelina, Texas,	101	Beaver Creek, Dakota,	
Antelope Creek, Oregon,	- 22	southwest part unorganized.	
Antietam Creek, West Va.,	- 21	Beaver Creek, Colorado,	- 4
Apishpa, Colorado,	- 17	Beaver Creek, Missouri,	101
Apalachicola, Florida,	- 9	Beaver Creek, Nebraska,	- 52
Apple Creek, Dakota,	- 20	Pawnee Indian Res.	
Applegate Creek, Oregon,	- 19	Beaver Creek, Texas,	- 5
Aransas, Texas,	164	Beaver, Dakota,	- 20
Aravaypa, Arizona,	- 5	Beaver, Minnesota,	- 6
Arkansas, Arkansas,	- 60	Beaver, New York,	- 6
Aroostooka, Maine,	- 1	Beaver, Oregon,	- 13
Arrow, Montana,	- 5	Bees Scies, Michigan,	- 20
Assiniboin Creek, Dakota,	- 39	Belle Fourche River, Dakota,	
Atahnam, Washington,	- 15	southwest part unorganized.	
Atascosa Creek, Texas,	154	Benito, California,	- 40
Atascaso, New Mexico,	11	B. Barren, Kentucky,	- 71
Atchafalaya, Louisiana,	- 41	Big Bear Creek, Alabama,	- 6
Au Sable, N. Y.,	- 3	Big Black, Mississippi,	- 49
		Big Cedar, Iowa,	- 89
Bad Land Creek, Dakota,	- 62	Big Creek, Indiana,	- 85
Bad, Dakota,	- 63	Big Creek, Louisiana,	- 14
Bad Water Creek, Wyoming,	- 2	Big Creek, Tennessee,	- 46
Baluarte Creek, Texas,	167	Big Dorcheat, Louisiana,	- 3
Bannack, Idaho,	- 10	Big Dry Creek, Montana,	- 6

ALPHABETICAL INDEX—RIVERS. 99

	Co.
Big Fork, Minnesota,	- 4
Big Hatchie, Tennessee,	- 50
Big Hole, Montana,	- 9
Big Horn, Montana,	- 11
Big Knife, Dakota,	- 11
Big Muddy, Montana,	- 6
Big Pigeon, Tennessee,	- 46
Big Salkchatchee, So. Carolina,	32
Big Sandy, Wyoming,	- 2
Big Sioux, Iowa,	- 32
Big Tarkis, Missouri,	- 11
Big Thompson Creek, Colorado,	4
Big White Face, Minnesota,	- 5
Big Wichita, Texas,	- 5
Bijou Creek, Colorado,	- 4
Bill Williams Fork, Arizona,	- 1
Biloxi, Mississippi,	- 71
Bitter Creek, Wyoming,	- 2
Bitter Creek, Wyoming,	- 5
Bitter Root, Montana,	- 1
Black Earth Creek, Dakota,	- 75
Black Fork, Texas,	- 27
Black Hawk Creek, Iowa,	- 40
Blackfoot Creek, Idaho,	- 10
Blackfoot, Montana,	- 1
Black, Arkansas,	- 60
Black, Maine,	- 1
Black, Michigan,	- 13
Black, Michigan,	- 57
Black, New York,	- 4
Black, Ohio,	- 10
Black, South Carolina,	- 25
Black, Wisconsin,	- 1
Black, Wisconsin,	- 27
Black Warrior Fork, Alabama,	- 18
Black Warrior River, Alabama,	- 31
Blackwater, Florida,	- 2
Blackwater, Virginia,	- 85
Blanchard Fork, Ohio,	- 4
Blanco Creek, Texas,	157
Blue, Indian Ter., Choctaw Nation.	
Blue, New Mexico,	- 13
Blue Stone, West Virginia,	- 50
Boeuf, Louisiana,	- 15
Bogue Chitto, Louisiana,	- 36
Bogue Homo Creek, Mississippi,	67
Boiling Creek, Colorado,	- 16
Bois d' Arc Creek, Texas,	- 14
Bois des Sioux, Dakota, Indian Reservation.	
Boisé, Idaho,	- 6
Boise, Wyoming,	- 5
Bonito, New Mexico,	- 11

	Co.
Booches Pool, Arizona,	- 2
Bosque, Texas,	- 68
Bourbeuse, Dakota,	- 30
Box Elder Creek, Dakota, southwest part unorganized.	
Boyer, Iowa,	- 70
Brady's Creek, Texas,	- 77
Branch Potomac, W. Virginia,	- 18
Brazos, Texas,	139
Brier Creek, Georgia,	- 83
Broad, South Carolina,	- 13
Bruneau, Idaho,	- 9
Brush Creek, Utah,	- 11
Buffalo Fork, Arkansas,	- 5
Buffalo, Minnesota,	- 2
Buffalo, Mississippi,	- 63
Buffalo, Tennessee,	- 30
Buffalo, Wisconsin,	- 18
Bull Run, Virginia,	- 7
Burnt Mt. Creek, Idaho,	- 9
Burnt, Oregon,	- 22
Butahatchee, Alabama,	- 23
Butte Creek, California,	- 14
Butte Creek, California,	- 3
Cache Creek, California,	- 22
Cache Creek, Indian Ter., Kiowas, Comanches, and Apaches.	
Cache, Arkansas,	- 43
Calaveras, California,	- 29
Calamas, Nebraska, Pawnee Indian Reservation.	
Calcasieu, Louisiana,	- 28
Caloosahatchee, Florida,	- 37
Canada Creek, N. Y.,	- 7
Canadian, Indian Ter., Choctaw Nation.	
Caney, Texas,	150
Canistes, New York,	- 40
Cannon Ball, Dakota,	- 19
Cannon Creek, Idaho,	- 9
Cannoachee, Georgia,	106
Canon, Minnesota,	- 59
Cape Fear, North Carolina,	- 93
Carson, Nevada,	- 8
Cass, Michigan,	- 47
Catawba, North Carolina,	- 70
Catfish Fork, Texas,	- 1
Catskill Creek, New York,	- 47
Cedar Creek, Texas,	- 53
Cedar Creek, Washington,	- 2
Cedar, Washington,	- 12
Chaco, New Mexico,	- 1

ALPHABETICAL INDEX—RIVERS.

River	Co.
Chahlat, Washington,	5
Chateaugay, New York,	2
Chattuga, Georgia,	10
Chariton, Missouri,	32
Chenning, Pennsylvania,	7
Cherana, Washington,	3
Cherry Creek, Dakota,	49
Cherry Creek, Wyoming,	5
Chickesawha, Mississippi,	68
Chipala, Florida,	7
Chippewa, Michigan,	47
Chitico, Oregon,	18
Chippewa, Wisconsin,	15
Choctawhatchee, Florida,	4
Chowan, North Carolina,	14
Chowchilla, California,	38
Chusea, New Mexico,	3
Chuma, New Mexico,	3
Cibolo Creek, Texas,	146
Clackamas, Oregon,	8
Clarion, Pennsylvania,	21
Clarke Fork, Montana,	10
Clear Boggy, Indian Ter.,	Choctaw Nation.
Clear Creek, Texas,	22
Clear Fork, Wyoming,	3
Clearwater, Idaho,	3
Cliff Creek, Oregon,	15
Clingwater Creek, Wyoming,	5
Clinch, Tennessee,	42
Coal, West Virginia,	42
Cloquet, Minnesota,	11
Coleto, Texas,	148
Cold Water, Mississippi,	17
Colorado, Texas,	150
Concho, Texas,	60
Conecuh, Florida,	1
Conewago Creek, Penn.,	60
Congaree, South Carolina,	22
Conhocton, New York,	40
Connecticut, Connecticut,	7
Coon, Iowa,	62
Coos, Oregon,	17
Coosa, Alabama,	14
Coquille, Oregon,	17
Corn Creek, Dakota, southwestern part unorganized.	
Cosumnes, California,	29
Cottonwood Creek, California,	41
Cottonwood Creek, Idaho,	3
Cottonwood Fork, Col'o River, Arizona,	2
Coyote Creek, California,	35

River	Co.
Cowhouse Creek, Texas,	80
Cow Pasture, Virginia,	22
Cowlitz, Washington,	18
Crazy Woman Creek, Wyom'g,	3
Crooked Fork, Missouri,	16
Crooked, Minnesota,	21
Crooked, Oregon,	13
Cross, Minnesota,	6
Crow Creek, Colorado,	4
Crow Creek, Dakota,	52
Crow, Minnesota,	38
Crow Wing, Minnesota,	9
Cumberland, Kentucky,	63
Current Creek, Wyoming,	2
Cuyahoga, Ohio,	11
Dan, Virginia,	91
Deep, North Carolina,	47
Deer Creek, California,	8
Deer Creek, Maryland,	7
Deer Creek, Mississippi,	43
Deer Creek, Wyoming,	5
Deer, Tennessee,	50
Delaware, Del., Del. Bay,	—
Delaware, (W. Br.,) N. Y.,	46
Delaware, (E. Br.) N. Y.,	46
Delaware Fork, Utah,	11
Denton Fork, Texas,	35
Des Arcs, Arkansas,	42
Des Chutes, Oregon,	13
Des Chutes, Washington,	13
Des Plaines, Illinois,	23
Dog Ears Creek, Dakota,	64
Double Mt. Fork, Texas,	17
Dry Creek, California,	51
Dry Creek, Wyoming,	5
Duchesne, Utah,	11
Duck, Tennessee,	30
Eagles Nest Creek, Dakota,	62
East Branch Feather, Cal.,	9
East Fork, San Carlos, Arizona,	2
East F'k, San Francisco, Arizona,	2
East Medicine, Dakota,	50
Econfeuce, Florida,	15
Edisto, South Carolina,	31
Eel, California,	4
Eel, Indiana,	62
Elder Creek, California,	8
Elk Creek, Dakota, southwest part unorganized.	
Elk Creek, Indian Ter., Creek Co.	
Elkhorn, Nebraska,	27

ALPHABETICAL INDEX—RIVERS.

River	Co.
Elk, West Virginia,	- 42
Elm Creek, Indian Ter., Kiowas, Comanches, and Apaches.	
Elm Creek, Texas,	142
Elm Fork, Texas,	- 11
Elm, Minnesota,	- 75
English, Iowa,	- 78
Enuoree, South Carolina,	- 13
Esopus Creek, N. Y.,	- 50
Fakauatchee, Florida,	- 38
Felix, New Mexico,	- 13
Fig, Virginia,	- 87
Finholloway, Florida,	- 15
Flambeux, Wisconsin,	- 7
Flat Creek, California,	- 43
Flat Head, Montana,	- 1
Flat, Missouri,	- 64
Flint, Alabama,	- 49
Floyds, Iowa,	- 32
Fourche Caddo, Arkansas,	- 57
Fourche la Fave, Arkansas,	- 39
Fossil F'k, San Fran., Arizona,	- 2
Fox, Illinois,	- 20
Franklin, Nevada,	- 3
French Broad, Tennessee,	- 44
Fresno Creek, California,	- 41
French Creek, Dakota, southwest part unorganized.	
Gallatin, Montana,	- 10
Gasconade, Missouri,	- 62
Gatas Creek, California,	- 41
Gauley, West Virginia,	- 48
Genesee, New York,	- 13
Gila, Arizona,	- 3
Godin's, Idaho,	- 8
Goose Creek, Idaho,	- 9
Goose Creek, Virginia,	- 63
Goose, Dakota,	- 18
Grand, Louisiana,	- 48
Grand, Michigan,	- 50
Grand, Missouri,	- 31
Grand, Ohio,	- 12
Grand Ronde, Washington,	- 22
Grass, New York,	- 1
Gravel Bottom F'k, Montana,	- 2
Great Auglaize, Missouri,	- 71
Great Blue, Indiana,	- 90
Great Falls, Montana,	- 5
Great Kanawha, West Va.,	- 32
Great Pedee, South Carolina,	- 25
Great Traverse, Michigan,	- 21

River	Co.
Green, Illinois,	- 17
Green, Kentucky,	- 42
Green, Utah,	- 17
Greenbriar, West Virginia,	- 50
Greenhorn, Colorado,	- 16
Grey Bull, Wyoming,	- 2
Gunnison, Colorado,	- 10
Guyandotte, West Virginia,	- 39
Hassayampa, Arizona,	- 4
Hat Creek, Dakota, southwest part unorganized.	
Hawk Creek, Florida,	- 36
Haw, North Carolina,	- 47
Heart, Dakota,	- 19
Hell Gate, Montana,	- 1
Henry's Fork, Idaho,	- 10
Henry's Fork, Wyoming,	- 2
Hiawassee, Tennessee,	- 93
Hicpotee, Virginia,	- 88
Hillsboro, Florida,	- 34
Honda Creek, Texas,	131
Homochitto, Mississippi,	- 56
Horse Creek, Wyoming,	- 5
Horsehead Creek, Dakota, southwest part unorganized.	
Horse Prairie Creek, Montana,	- 8
Horse Shoe Creek, Wyoming,	- 5
Hot Spring Creek, Montana,	- 1
Housatonic, Conn.,	- 5
Hudson, New York,	- 56
Huerfano, Colorado,	- 16
Humboldt, Nevada,	- 8
Huron, Ohio,	- 9
Hy-os-kwa-ha-loos, Washington,	2
Illinois, Illinois,	- 58
Illinois, Oregon,	- 18
Independence Creek, Texas,	- 60
Indian Creek, Oregon,	- 21
Indian, Florida,	- 30
Indian, New York,	- 1
Iowa, Iowa,	- 79
Iron, Wisconsin,	- 2
Island Creek, West Virginia,	- 9
Jaboncilles Creek, Texas,	163
Jacks Fork, Missouri,	- 89
James, or Dakota, Dakota,	- 81
James, Missouri,	- 99
James, Virginia,	- 73
Jefferson, Montana,	- 10
Jocko, Montana,	- 1

ALPHABETICAL INDEX—RIVERS.

River	Co.
John Days, Oregon,	13
Johns Creek, Virginia,	43
Jordan, Oregon,	22
Judith, Montana,	5
Kalamazoo, Michigan,	58
Kankakee, Illinois,	23
Kaskaskia, Illinois,	87
Kaweah Creek, California,	43
Keg Creek, Iowa,	80
Kelseys, California,	4
Kentucky, Kentucky,	14
Kennebec, Maine,	14
Kern, California,	45
Kettle Creek, Pennsylvania,	15
Kettle, Minnesota,	21
Keya Paha, Nebraska,	2
Kianashi, Indian Ter., Choctaw Nation.	
Kickapoo, Wisconsin,	40
Kings, California,	41
Kiowa Creek, Colorado,	4
Kissimee, Florida,	36
Klamath, California,	1
Klikitat, Washington,	21
Lacqui Parle, Minnesota,	44
Lake Fork, Texas,	40
Lake Fork, Utah,	11
Lampasas, Texas,	80
Lates Lengua Creek, Texas,	58
Lava Creek, Arizona,	2
Lavaca, Texas,	159
Leaf, Minnesota,	15
Leon Creek, Texas,	132
Leon, Texas,	95
Lewis, Washington,	19
Little, Arkansas,	21
Little, South Carolina,	18
Little Arkansas, Kansas,	73
Little Black, Maine,	1
Little Calcasieu, Louisiana,	28
Little Colorado, or Flax, Arizona,	2
Little Eau Plein, Wisconsin,	22
Little Fork, Minnesota,	4
Little Humboldt, Nevada,	2
Little Miami, Ohio,	79
Little Missouri, Arkansas,	64
Little Missouri, Dakota,	9
Little Muddy Creek, Dakota,	1
Little Pedee, South Carolina,	25
Little Pigeon Creek, Indiana,	87
Little Porcupine, Montana,	11
Little Red, Arkansas,	30
Little Salmon, Idaho,	5
Little Shyenne, Dakota,	39
Little Sioux, Iowa,	44
Little Tennessee, Tenn.,	43
Little Wabash, Illinois,	80
Little Wichita, Texas,	9
Lizard, Iowa,	36
Llano, Texas,	92
Locust Fork, Alabama,	19
Lodge Pole Creek, Nebraska,	28
Logan Creek, Nebraska,	4
Long Lake Creek, Dakota,	20
Long Prairie, Minnesota,	16
Loop Fork, Nebraska,	20
Lost, Oregon,	20
Lost, West Virginia,	19
Lumber, North Carolina,	87
Lycoming Creek, Penn.,	16
Lynches Creek, S. Carolina,	24
Mable, Montana,	1
McArthur, Idaho,	8
McCloud, California,	6
Machias, Maine,	10
Mackenzie's Fork, Oregon,	12
Mad, California,	4
Madison, Montana,	10
Magalloway, Maine,	5
Mahoming Creek, Penn.,	22
Malade, Idaho,	8
Malade, Utah,	1
Malheur, Oregon,	22
Manatee, Florida,	37
Manedowish, Wisconsin,	7
Manistee, Michigan,	26
Maple, Iowa,	44
Maple, Dakota,	27
Maple, Michigan,	52
Maquoketa, Iowa,	55
Marais des Cyanes, Missouri,	66
Marias, Montana,	5
Mariposa, California,	38
Marquette, Michigan,	32
Marsh, Minnesota,	2
Matapony, Virginia,	32
Mattawamkeag, Maine,	4
Maumee, Ohio,	3
Mayo, North Carolina,	5
Meadow, West Virginia,	44
Medicine Bow Creek, Wyoming,	3
Medina, Texas,	146
Medicine, Dakota,	64

ALPHABETICAL INDEX—RIVERS. 103

River	Co.
Meherrin, North Carolina,	13
Menomonee, Michigan,	8
Meramec, Missouri,	63
Merced, California,	38
Merrimac, Massachusetts,	7
Methow, Washington,	2
Miami, Ohio,	79
Michigamme, Michigan,	8
Middle Fork, Oregon,	12
Middle, Indian Ter., N. W. part.	
Middle, Iowa,	74
Middle, Virginia,	10
Middle Boggy, Indian Ter., Choctaw Nation.	
Middle Branch, Kansas,	19
Middle Coon, Iowa,	61
Middle Fork, Deer, Tenn.,	27
Miembres, New Mexico,	12
Milk, Montana,	6
Mill Creek, California,	8
Minnesota, Minnesota,	51
Miry Fork, Montana,	2
Mission, Texas,	157
Missisquoi, Vermont,	2
Mississippi, Louisiana,	56
Mizpah Creek, Montana,	11
Mobile, Alabama,	58
Mohave, California,	50
Mohawk, New York,	20
Mohican, Ohio,	45
Mokelumne, California,	29
Molalle, Oregon,	8
Monocacy, Maryland,	4
Monongahela, Penn.,	34
Montreal, Wisconsin,	3
Moose, Maine,	2
Moose, New York,	6
Mormon, Idaho,	5
Moro, Arkansas,	65
Mora, New Mexico,	7
Moreau, Dakota,	39
Morse's Creek, Dakota,	56
Muddy Creek, Indian Ter., Chickasaw Nation.	
Muddy, Dakota,	43
Muskegon, Michigan,	44
Muskingum, Ohio,	78
Mussel Shell, Montana,	6
Nacimiento Creek, Cal.,	40
Nachess, Washington,	15
Namikagon, Wisconsin,	4
Napa, California,	21
Navarro, California,	10
Navasota, Texas,	96
Navidad, Texas,	149
Nechez, Texas,	127
Nehalem, Oregon,	3
Nenelaw, Michigan,	19
Neosho, Indian Ter., Cherokee Reservation.	
Neuse, North Carolina,	83
Neversink, New York,	52
New, California,	51
New, Virginia,	60
Niagara, New York,	11
Niobrara, Nebraska,	2
Nisanally, Washington,	13
Nodaway, Missouri,	11
Nokay, Minnesota,	18
Noksahk, Washington,	1
Nolechucky, Tennessee,	46
North, Iowa,	74
North Anna, Virginia,	29
North Branch, Nebraska,	21
North Branch, Bitter Creek, Wyoming,	2
North Branch, Shyenne, Wyoming,	5
North Tabins, Missouri,	24
North Fork, S. Carolina,	28
North Fork Canadian, Indian Ter., Creek Country.	
North F'k Cannon Ball, Dakota,	19
North Fork Clearwater, Idaho,	3
North Fork Deer, Tenn.,	27
North Fork Green, Utah,	11
North Fork, Indian Ter., Kiowas, Comanches, and Apaches.	
North Fork Kern, California,	45
North Fork Platte, Nebraska,	30
North Nishuabatony, Iowa,	91
North Fork Santiam, Oregon,	11
North Fork Shenandoah, Va.,	5
North Umpqua, Oregon,	16
Nottoway, North Carolina,	13
Nueces, Texas,	163
Oak Creek, Dakota,	63
Oak Creek, Texas,	61
Obion, Tennessee,	26
Ocate, New Mexico,	4
Ocilla, Florida,	13
Ocklockonee, Florida,	12
Ocmulgee, Georgia,	115
Ocoee, Tennessee,	93

ALPHABETICAL INDEX—RIVERS.

	Co.		Co.
Oconee, Georgia,	104	Petit Jean, Arkansas,	28
Oconto, Wisconsin,	9	Pey, or Elm, Dakota,	34
Ocoqua, Virginia,	7	Piedernales, Texas,	108
Octawaha, Florida,	26	Pinal Creek, Arizona,	2
Ogeechee, Georgia,	106	Pierres Creek, Idaho,	10
Ohio, Kentucky,	63	Pine Creek, Pennsylvania,	16
Oil Creek, Pennsylvania,	11	Piny Creek, Missouri,	73
Okinakane, Washington,	2	Piscataquis, Maine,	4
Okobaja Creek, Dakota,	40	Pisco, Washington,	21
Olmos Creek, Texas,	168	Platte, Nebraska,	27
Orange Creek, Florida,	26	Pocotaligo, W. Virginia,	42
Oraytayous, Washington,	3	Poison Spring Creek, Wyom'g,	3
Oro Fino Creek, Idaho,	4	Pomme de Terre, Minnesota,	34
Osa Creek, Arizona,	2	Pommes des Terres, Missouri,	57
Osage, Missouri,	60	Ponka Creek, Dakota,	62
Oswegatchie, New York,	1	Ponka, Dakota,	79
Oswego, New York,	5	Porcupine, Montana,	11
Ottawa, Ohio,	3	Porcupine Tail Creek, Dakota,	
Otter Creek, Vermont,	8	southwest part unorganized.	
Owens, California,	46	Portage, Ohio,	7
Owhyhee, Oregon,	22	Porte Neuf, Idaho,	10
Owl Creek, Wyoming,	2	Posey Creek, California,	45
		Poteau, Indian Ter.,	
Pah Ute Creek, California,	50		Choctaw Nation.
Pajaro, California,	40	Potomac, Maryland,	19
Palo Blanco Creek, Texas,	167	Powder, Montana,	11
Paloose, Washington,	3	Powder, Oregon,	15
Pamunkey, Virginia,	53	Prieto Creek, Texas,	152
Papo Aigre, Wyoming,	2	Puerco, New Mexico,	10
Panoche Creek, California,	41	Purgatory, Colorado,	17
Panther Creek, Ky.,	43	Putah Creek, California,	22
Parke Creek, Arizona,	2		
Park, Dakota,	7	Quarrel Creek, Montana,	6
Pascagoula, Mississippi,	72	Quillehyats, Washington,	4
Pashamaran, Idaho,	8	Quinaintte, Washington,	8
Passadumkeag, Maine,	4	Quius, Nevada,	2
Pass Creek, Dakota,	62		
Pass d' Aro Fork, Texas,	37	Racket, New York,	1
Patsaliga, Alabama,	61	Raft Creek, Idaho,	9
Patterson's Creek, W. Va.,	18	Rapid Creek, Dakota,	
Patuxent, Maryland,	19	southwest part unorganized.	
Pawnee Fork, Kansas,	69	Rapid Ann, Virginia,	15
Paw Paw, Michigan,	71	Rappahannock, Virginia,	37
Payette Creek, Idaho,	6	Raw Hide Creek, Wyoming,	5
Pearl, Mississippi,	70	Ready Fork, N. Carolina,	24
Pea River, Alabama,	63	Red Creek, Indian Ter., Osage Res.	
Pease Creek, Florida,	37	Red, Louisiana,	27
Pembina, Dakota,	7	Red of the North, West Minn.,	
Penasco, New Mexico,	13	empties into Lake Winnepeg, B. C.	
Pennigenassett, N. H.,	2	Red, Minnesota,	12
Penobscot, Maine,	8	Red, Wisconsin,	3
Penobscot, (W. Br.,) Maine,	2	Red Cedar, Iowa,	79
Peshtigo, Wisconsin,	9	Red Cedar, Wisconsin,	14

ALPHABETICAL INDEX—RIVERS.

River	Co.
Red Fork, Texas,	60
Red Lake, Minnesota,	2
Redwood Creek, California,	2
Red Wood, Minnesota,	54
Reed Creek, California,	8
Ree, or Grande, Dakota,	29
Reelfoot, Tennessee,	26
Reese, Nevada,	9
Republican, Kansas,	39
Reynolds Creek, Idaho,	9
Rifle, Michigan,	42
Rio Bonita, Arizona,	2
Rio de Chelle, Arizona,	2
Rio de Chelle, Utah,	20
Rio de los Dolores, Colorado,	10
Rio Frio, Texas,	154
Rio Leona, Texas,	143
Rio Wutroso, Arizona,	5
Rio Pecos, Texas,	60
Rio Prieto, Arizona,	2
Rio Puerco of the West, Arizona,	2
Rio Salado, or Salt, Arizona,	4
Rio San Domingo, Arizona,	5
Rio San Pedro, Arizona,	5
Rio San Pedro, Texas,	60
Rio Santa Cruz, Arizona,	5
Rivanna, Virginia,	27
River Au Sable, Michigan,	31
Riviere des Lacs, Dakota,	3
Roanoke, North Carolina,	31
Rock Creek, Idaho,	5
Rock, Illinois,	15
Rock, Ohio,	11
Rocky, North Carolina,	85
Rogue, Oregon,	18
Rondout Creek, New York,	50
Rosebud, Montana,	11
Rough Creek, Kentucky,	78
Rum, Minnesota,	39
Rush Creek, Colorado,	13
Rush, Dakota,	27
Russian, California,	19
Sabinal Creek, Texas,	131
Sabine, Louisiana,	37
Sac, Missouri,	66
Saco, Maine,	11
Sacramento, California,	24
San Antonio, Texas,	157
St. Bernard, Texas,	139
St. Croix, Wisconsin,	13
St. Croix, Maine,	10
St. Felipe Creek, Cal.,	51

River	Co.
San Jacinto, Texas,	125
St. Fernando Creek, Texas,	163
St. Francis, Arkansas,	45
St. Francis, Maine,	1
St. Johns, Florida,	22
St. Johns, (W. Br.,) Maine,	1
St. Josephs, Idaho,	1
St. Josephs, Michigan,	71
St. Louis, Wisconsin,	1
St. Marys, Georgia,	136
St. Peters, Dakota, Indian Res.	
St. Regis, New York,	2
St. Regis, Montana,	1
St. Vrains Fork, Wyoming,	2
Sage Creek, Wyoming,	2
Saginaw, Michigan,	42
Salado, New Mexico,	11
Salinas, California,	40
Saline Bayou, Louisiana,	18
Saline Creek, Illinois,	99
Saline Creek, Indian Ter., Cherokee Reservation.	
Saline, Arkansas,	65
Saline, Kansas,	36
Saline, Louisiana,	22
Salitz, Oregon,	3
Salmon, Idaho,	3
Salmon, Maine,	11
Salmon, New York,	2
Salmon Fall, Idaho,	9
Salt Creek, Indiana,	72
Salt Fork, Indian Ter., Kiowas, Comanches, and Apaches.	
Salt Fork, Texas,	17
Salt, Dakota,	7
Salt, Missouri,	42
Salt, Wyoming,	3
Saluda, South Carolina,	20
Samish, Washington,	1
San Carlos, Arizona,	2
Sand, Minnesota,	21
Sanders Creek, Texas,	14
Sandies Creek, Texas,	147
Sandusky, Ohio,	8
Sandy Creek, Colorado,	17
Sandy Lick Creek, Penn.,	22
Sandy, Maine,	2
San Francisco, Arizona,	2
San Francisco, Texas,	58
San Gabriel, Texas,	95
Sangamon, Illinois,	45
San Jose, New Mexico,	9
San Joaquin, California,	29

ALPHABETICAL INDEX—RIVERS.

River	Co.
San Marcos, Texas,	134
San Miguel Creek, Texas,	153
San Saba, Texas,	77
Sans Bois Creek, Indian Ter., Choctaw Nation.	
Santa Anna, California,	49
Santa Clara, California,	48
Santa Fe, Florida,	17
Santa Inez, California,	47
Santa Maria, Arizona,	1
Santa Maria, California,	47
Santa Petronala, Texas,	163
Sappa Creek, Nebraska,	53
Saranac, New York,	3
Satilla, Georgia,	118
Sauk, Minnesota,	28
Savannah, Georgia,	107
Schoharia, New York,	32
Schuylkill, Pennsylvania,	65
Scioto, Ohio,	84
Sevier, Utah,	14
Sheboygan, Michigan,	13
Shell, Wyoming,	2
Shell Rock, Iowa,	29
Sherlon's Fork, Arizona,	2
Shiawasee, Michigan,	47
Shiloh, Louisiana,	6
Shyenne, Dakota,	27
Simmons Fork, North Carolina,	74
Skunk, Iowa,	100
Shokomish, Washington,	10
Skagit, Washington,	1
Sipsey, Alabama,	23
Sipsey Fork, Alabama,	18
Slate, Virginia,	46
Slippery Rock Creek, Penn.,	19
Smith, North California,	5
Smith's Fork, Nebraska,	28
Smith, California,	1
Smith's, Montana,	7
Smith's, Oregon,	16
Smoke, Washington,	3
Smoky Hill Fork, Kansas,	29
Snake, Idaho,	10
Snake, Minnesota,	21
Snake, Nebraska, west of,	1
Snohomish, Washington,	7
Soasahatchie, Tennessee,	77
Soldier, Iowa,	57
Solomons Fork, Kansas,	19
South, Iowa,	74
South, North Carolina,	93
South, Virginia,	10

River	Co.
South Anna, Virginia,	29
South Branch, Nebraska,	20
South Br. Shenandoah, W. Va.,	21
South Coon, Iowa,	61
South Fabins, Missouri,	24
South Fork White, Dakota,	63
South Fork, Oregon,	13
South Fork, South Carolina,	28
South Fork, Texas,	1
South Fork, Texas,	27
South Fork Deer, Tennessee,	50
South Fork Eel, California,	10
South Fork Humboldt, Nevada,	3
South Fork Malheur, Oregon,	22
South Fork Pease, Texas,	5
South Fork Platte, Nebraska,	30
S. F. Santiam, Oregon,	11
South Umpqua, Oregon,	16
South Yadkin, North Carolina,	43
Spavina Creek, Indian Ter., Choctaw Reservation.	
Spanish, Utah,	10
Spokane, Washington,	2
Spoon, Illinois,	18
Sprague, Oregon,	20
Spring Creek, Arkansas,	9
Spring Creek, Dakota, southwest part unorganized.	
Spring Creek, Texas,	125
Squirrel Creek, Colorado,	16
Staluk Whamish, Washington,	7
Stanislaus, California,	36
Staunton, Virginia,	91
Steinhatchee, Florida,	18
Stevens Creek, South Carolina,	19
Stinking, Wyoming,	2
Stony Creek, California,	12
Strong, Mississippi,	51
Sugar Creek, Indiana,	44
Sugar Creek, Ohio,	46
Sulphur Spring Creek, Wyom'g,	2
Sun Flower, Mississippi,	38
Susan, California,	7
Susquehanna, Maryland,	7
Susquehanna, (W. Br.,) Penn.,	26
Susquehanna, (E. Br.,) Penn.,	27
Suwanee, Florida,	28
Swan, Missouri,	101
Sweet Water, Wyoming,	3
Swift Creek, Virginia,	50
Swift, North Carolina,	29
Swoolamish, Washington,	1
Sybilles Fork, Wyoming,	5

LPB

ALPHABETICAL INDEX—RIVERS.

	Co.		Co.
Tallapoosa, Alabama,	- 44	Ushkabwaka, Minnesota,	- 5
Tallahala Creek, Mississippi,	- 67		
Tallala, Georgia,	- 10	Vermillion Creek, Dakota,	- 82
Tallahatchie, Mississippi,	- 8	Vermillion River, Minnesota,	- 5
Tamarac, Minnesota,	- 1	Vernon Fork, Indiana,	- 73
Tanawha, West Virginia,	- 22	Virgin, Nevada,	- 15
Tangipahoa, Louisiana,	- 34		
Tar, North Carolina,	- 53	Wabash, Illinois,	- 95
Taylor's Bayou, Texas,	127	Waccamaw, South Carolina,	- 25
Temperance, Minn.,	- 6	Walker, Nevada,	- 13
Tennessee, Kentucky,	- 90	Wallahalla, California,	- 19
Teusas, Louisiana,	- 22	Wallkill Creek, New York,	- 50
Terrapin Creek, Colorado,	- 4	Walnut Creek, Indian Ter.,	
Teton, Montana,	- 5	Chickasaw Nation.	
Thief, Minnesota,	- 2	Walnut Creek, Iowa,	- 91
Thunder Bay, Michigan,	- 19	Walnut Creek, Kansas,	- 51
Tia Juana, California,	- 51	Wandushkaw, or Snake, Dakota,	43
Tickfaw, Louisiana,	- 45	Wapsipinicon, Iowa,	- 69
Tide Creek, Dakota,	- 9	Washita, Indian Ter.,	
Tiffin, Ohio,	- 4	Chickasaw Nation.	
Trinoanogos, Utah,	- 10	Washita, Louisiana,	- 22
Timpas Creek, Colorado,	- 17	Wateree, South Carolina,	- 22
Tippecanoe, Indiana,	- 29	Waterhole Creek, Dakota,	- 64
Tobacco, Montana,	- 1	Weber, Utah,	- 4
Tombigby, Alabama,	- 49	Wenatshapan, Washington,	- 15
Tongue, Montana,	- 11	West, Vermont,	- 14
Toreau, Louisiana,	- 17	West Branch White, Ind.,	- 69
Toyah Creek, Texas,	- 59	West Fork, Louisiana,	- 28
Tradewater, Kentucky,	- 41	West Fork, Indian Ter.,	
Trempealeau, Wisconsin,	- 18	Kiowas, Comanches, and Apaches.	
Trent, North Carolina,	- 82	West Fork, Texas,	- 35
Trinity, California,	- 2	West Fork Cedar, Iowa,	- 29
Trinity, Texas,	126	West Fork Little Sioux, Ky.,	- 44
Truckee, Nevada,	- 5	West Fork Sandy, Ky.,	- 11
Tugaloo, South Carolina,	- 18	West Fork Shyenne, Wyoming,	5
Tug Fork Sandy, Ky.,	- 24	Whetstone, Ohio,	- 55
Tulare, California,	- 43	White, Arkansas,	- 19
Tunicho, New Mexico,	- 3	White, Dakota,	- 64
Tuolumne, California,	- 36	White, Indiana,	- 69
Turkey Creek, Arizona,	- 4	White, Utah,	- 11
Turkey, Iowa,	- 31	White, Washington,	- 12
Turtle, Dakota,	- 18	White, Wisconsin,	- 3
Turtle, Dakota,	- 44	White Earth Creek, Dakota,	
Tuscarawas, Ohio,	- 46	southwest part unorganized.	
Two Battle Creek, Kansas,	- 65	White Earth, Dakota,	- 2
Tygarts Valley, West Va.,	- 6	Wild Rice, Minnesota,	- 2
		Willamette, Oregon,	- 7
Umatilla, Oregon,	- 14	Willis, Virginia,	- 47
Umpqua, Oregon,	- 16	Willopah, Washington,	- 9
Union, Maine,	- 9	Willow Creek, Oregon,	- 13
Upper Iowa, Iowa,	- 11	Willow, Minnesota,	- 10
Upper Knife, Dakota,	- 2	Wind, Wyoming,	- 2
Upper Yakima, Washington,	- 15	Winooski, Vermont,	- 5

ALPHABETICAL INDEX—CAPES.

	Co.		Co.
Winter Road, Minnesota,	1	Yazoo, Mississippi,	43
Wisconsin, Wisconsin,	40	Yegua Creek, Texas,	111
Wiser Creek, Idaho,	6	Yellow, Alabama,	61
Withlacoochee, Florida,	16	Yellow, Florida,	2
Withlockoochee, Florida,	28	Yellow, Wisconsin,	4
Wolf Creek, Nebraska,	53	Yellow, Wisconsin,	29
Wolf, Mississippi,	71	Yellow Medicine, Minn.,	43
Wolf, Wisconsin,	34	Yellow Stone, Montana,	6
Wounded Knee Creek, Dakota, southwest part unorganized.		Yellow Water Creek, Montana,	6
		Yockanockany's Creek, Miss.,	40
Whisky Creek, Wyoming,	4	Yoconey, Missssssippi,	17
		Youghogheny, Penn.,	34
Yadkin, North Carolina,	43	Yuba, California,	15
Yakima, Washington,	21		
Yallabusha, Mississippi,	24	Zumbro, Minnesota,	60
Yamhill Fork, Oregon,	5	Zuni, Arizona,	2
Yampa Creek, Arizona,	1		

CAPES.

	Co.		Co.
Cape Ann, Mass.,	7	Little Point Ausable, Mich.,	37
Cape Arago, Oregon,	17		
Cape Blanco, Oregon,	18	Montauk Point, L. I.,	60
Cape Canaveral, Florida,	30		
Cape Charles, Maryland,	40	North Point, Michigan,	19
Cape Cod, Massachusetts,	12		
Cape Disappointment, Wash'n,	9	Pemmaquid Point, Maine,	15
Cape Elizabeth, Maine,	12	Point Adams, Oregon,	1
Cape Fear, North Carolina,	93	Point Arena, California,	10
Cape Flattery, Washington,	4	Point Arquilla, California,	47
Cape Florida, Florida,	39	Point aux Bees Scies, Mich.,	20
Cape Foulweather, Oregon,	3	Point Bonita, California,	20
Cape Hatteras, N. C.,	54	Point Brown, Washington,	8
Cape Henlopen, Delaware,	3	Point Conception, Cal.,	47
Cape Henry, Virginia,	99	Point De Los Reyes, Cal.,	20
Cape Lookout, N. Carolina,	91	Point Gordo, Cal.,	40
Cape Lookout, Oregon,	3	Point Lobos, Cal.,	27
Cape May, New Jersey,	21	Point Pinos, Cal.,	40
Cape Mendocino, California,	4	Point Sur, California,	40
Cape Perpetua, Oregon,	12	Point Vincent, Cal.,	49
Cape Romano, Florida,	38		
Cape Romain, S. Carolina,	30	Racoon Point, Lousiana,	54
Cape Sable, Florida,	39		
Cape San Blas, Florida,	7	Southwest Cape, Florida,	12
False Cape, California,	4	Tawas Point, Michigan,	31
False Fillamook, Oregon,	1	Tillamook Head, Oregon,	1
Fletcher Neck, Maine,	11	Toke Point, Washington,	9
Gravelly Point, Michigan,	42	Umpqua Head, Oregon,	16
Great Point Ausable, Mich.,	32		
		White Fish Point, Mich.,	6
Heweena Point, Mich.,	3		

BAYS.

	Co.		Co.
Admiralty Inlet, Washington,	5	Juan de Fuca Strait, Wash'n,	4
Albemarle Sound, northeast coast North Carolina.		Jupiter Inlet, Florida,	36
Appalachee, Florida,	13	Laguna Madre, Texas,	168
Atchafalaya, Louisiana,	47	Lampa, Florida,	34
		Little Egg Harbor, N. J.,	14
Barataria, Louisiana,	55	L. I. Sound, south of Conn.,	—
Barnegat Inlet, New Jersey,	15		
Barnegat, New Jersey,	15	Massachusetts, Mass.,	8
Barnes Sound, Florida,	39	Matanzas Inlet, Florida,	27
Bay Ronde, Louisiana,	56	Matagorda, Texas,	150
Bear Harbor, California,	10	Mississippi Sound, Miss.,	71
Bellingham, Washington,	1	Mobile, Alabama,	59
Biscayne, Florida,	20	Monterey, California,	40
Bodega, California,	39	Musquito Inlet, Florida,	30
Boundary, Washington,	1		
Bulls, South Carolina,	30	Narraguagus, Maine,	10
Buzzards, Mass.,	12	Narragansett, R. I.,	5
		Nekas, Oregon,	3
Camels, California,	40	New River Inlet, Florida,	39
Cote Blanche, Louisiana,	47		
Chandeleur Sound, S. E. La.,	—	Ocracoke Inlet, E. Pamlico Sound, North Carolina coast.	
Charlotte Harbor, Florida,	37		
Chatham, Florida,	39	Oregon Inlet, E. coast N. Carolina.	
Chesapeake, Maryland,	—	Oyster, Louisiana,	56
Chincoteague, Maryland,	23	Oyster, Florida,	39
Cove Sound, North Carolina,	91		
Corpus Christi, Texas,	163	Pamlico, North Carolina,	53
Crystal, Florida,	31	Pamlico Sound, N. Carolina,	54
		Peconic, Long Island,	60
Delaware, east of Delaware,	—	Pelican, California,	1
		Penobscot, Maine,	8
East, Texas,	126	Pensacola, Florida,	2
Estero, California,	44	Pugets Sound, Washington,	14
Florida, Florida,	39	Rosario Strait, Washington,	1
Florida Strait, Florida, south,	—		
Fon du Lac, Wisconsin,	1	St. Andre, Florida,	5
Frenchman, Maine,	9	San Antonio, Texas,	158
		San Luis, California,	44
Galveston, Texas,	140	San Pablo, California,	20
Green, Wisconsin,	11	Saginaw, Michigan,	43
		Sarasota, Florida,	37
Half Moon, California,	32	Shoalwater, Washington,	9
Hatteras Inlet, E. Pamlico Sound, North Carolina Coast.		South, Long Island,	60
		Strait of Mackinaw, Michigan,	11
Hood's Canal, Washington,	5	Suisun, California,	23
Humboldt, California,	4		
		Teaqumenen, Michigan,	6
Indian Inlet, Florida,	36	Terrebonne, Louisiana,	54
Isle au Breton Sound, S. E. La.,	—	Thunder, Michigan,	19

ALPHABETICAL INDEX—ISLANDS.

	Co.
Tillamook, Oregon,	3
Vermillion, Louisiana,	- 38
Vineyard Sound, Mass.,	- 13

	Co.
West, Texas,	140
West, Louisiana,	- 56
White Water, Florida,	- 39
Winyah, South Carolina,	- 25

ISLANDS.

	Co.
Amelia, Florida,	- 21
Anastasia, Florida,	- 27
Apostle, Wisconsin,	- 2
Big Beaver, Michigan,	- 10
Block, Rhode Island,	- 4
Bois Blanc, Michigan,	- 13
Breton, Louisiana,	- 56
Caman's, Washington,	- 6
Campobell's, Maine,	- 10
Captive, Florida,	- 37
Cat, Mississippi,	- 71
Cedar, North Carolina,	- 91
Chandeleur, Miss., south of,	- 71
Charity, Michigan,	- 43
Cooper's, South Carolina,	- 30
Cumberland, Georgia,	136
Dauphin, Alabama,	- 58
Deer, Maine,	- 10
Derniere, Louisiana,	- 54
Dry Tortugas, Florida,	- 39
Edisto, South Carolina,	- 31
Elizabeth, Mass.,	- 10
Farallone's, California,	- 20
Fisher's, Connecticut,	- 8
Florida Keys, Florida,	- 39
Fox, Michigan,	- 10
Galveston, Texas,	140
Gardiner's, New York,	- 60
Gasparilla, Florida,	- 37
Grand Crozier, La., east of,	- 56
Grand Menan, Maine,	- 10
Haut Isle, Maine,	- 9
Hilton Head, South Carolina,	- 32
Horn, Mississippi,	- 72
Jekyl, Georgia,	119
Kelley's, Ohio,	- 9
Key West, Florida,	- 39

	Co.
Kiawah, South Carolina,	- 30
Lacosta, Florida,	- 37
Long, New York,	58, 59 & 60
Long, Texas,	168
Long Key, Florida,	- 37
Lopez, Washington,	- 1
Machias Seal, Maine,	- 10
Madeleine, Wisconsin,	- 2
Manitou, Michigan,	- 10
Marquesas Key, Florida,	- 39
Marsh Island, Louisiana,	- 47
Martha's Vineyard, Mass.,	- 13
Matagorda, Texas,	159
Matinicus, Maine,	- 16
Merritt's, Florida,	- 30
Michigan, Wisconsin,	- 2
Middle, Michigan,	- 14
Mt. Desert, Maine,	- 9
Nantucket, Mass.,	- 14
Orcas, Washington,	- 1
Ossabaw, Georgia,	106
Outer, Wisconsin,	- 2
Palm Key, Florida,	- 37
Petit Bois, Alabama,	- 58
Pine Key, Florida,	- 34
Presqu Isle, Wisconsin,	- 2
Pte Pelée, Ohio,	- 9
Roanoke, North Carolina,	- 34
Ross, Maine,	- 10
St. George's, Florida,	- 9
St. Simon's, Georgia,	119
Sanibal, Florida,	- 37
San Miguel, California,	- 48
Santa Barbara, California,	- 49
Santa Cruz, California,	- 48
Santa Catalina, California,	- 49
San Clemente, California,	- 51
San Juan, Washington,	- 1
San Nicholas, California,	- 49

ALPHABETICAL INDEX—ISLANDS.

	Co.		Co.
Santa Rosa, California,	48	Tatoosh, Washington,	4
Santa Rosa, Florida,	2	Tybee, Georgia,	107
Sapelo, Georgia,	120		
Ship Island, Mississippi,	71	Whidbey's, Washington,	6
South Anclote, Florida,	31	Whitehead, Maine,	10
Swan's Island, Maine,	9	Wolfe, New York,	4